Murray &
Catherine Stiller

Dear Murray & Catherine

You two are so loved.
Your lives & vision continue to
inspire me.
          Quite a journey!

          Love, Dad / Brian

FIND A BROKEN WALL

7 *Ancient Principles* *for 21st Century Leaders*

find a
BROKEN
WALL

7 ANCIENT PRINCIPLES for
21st century LEADERS

BRIAN C. STILLER

CASTLE QUAY BOOKS

Find a Broken Wall: 7 Ancient Principles for 21st Century Leaders

Copyright ©2012 Brian C Stiller
All rights reserved
Printed in Canada
International Standard Book Number: 978-1-927355-02-2 (hard cover)
ISBN soft cover: 978-1-894860-42-0
ISBN 978-1-927355-80-2 EPUB

Published by:
Castle Quay Books
1307 Wharf Street, Pickering, Ontario, L1W 1A5
Tel: (416) 573-3249
E-mail: info@castlequaybooks.com
www.castlequaybooks.com

Edited by Audrey Dorsch and Marina Hofman-Willard
Cover design by Burst Impressions
Printed at Transcontinental Printing, Canada

Library and Archives Canada Cataloguing in Publication
Stiller, Brian C.
        Find a broken wall [electronic resource] : 7 ancient principles for 21st century leaders / Brian C. Stiller.

Includes bibliographical references and index.
Electronic monograph issued in PDF format.
Also issued in print format.
ISBN 978-1-894860-02-2

        1. Leadership. 2. Leadership—Religious aspects—Christianity. I. Title. II. Title: Seven ancient principles

for 21st century leaders.

HM1261.S748 2012   303.3'4   C2012-901719-1

Dedication

To those who over my lifetime have enabled me by their
friendship and support in leading local and national ministries

The heart of leadership is the heart of the leader. Partly visionary, partly turn-around artist and master strategist, Brian Stiller offers a compelling insight into the heart of a leader—his own heart. *Find a Broken Wall* is both a gripping story and an insightful challenge from a man who has seen beyond the "lost cause" of faltering organizations to champion the cause of rebuilding, restoring, and reinvigorating.

Ron Nikkel, President and CEO
Prison Fellowship International

Through personal transparency and provocative insights, Brian Stiller tells a refreshing story of Nehemiah that all of us in leadership need to hear and heed. Since I know Brian as a friend, the best part of reading this book is understanding that the man who wrote these words also strives from his heart to live these words. If you want your vision stoked, take the time to savour this book forged on the anvil of Brian's own effective and servant-hearted life of leadership.

Barry H. Corey, President
Biola University

Deeply personal and remarkably insightful, *Find a Broken Wall* will call the leader out of every reader. Brian's fascinating and sometimes difficult journey in leadership will encourage, inspire and challenge both seasoned and emerging leaders. Read this and let it spur you on to find the broken walls that God is calling you to rebuild.

Dave Toycen, President and CEO
World Vision Canada

I kid Brian about how he gets in touch with his "inner locomotive." This "locomotive," fuelled by his passionate faith in Christ, shapes and motivates his leadership of difficult causes. His remarkable vision for rebuilding valuable Kingdom resources has led him on a costly but fruitful leadership track. This book gives us a window into his inner locomotive and encourages us with the wisdom of proven experience to engage in the difficult task of leadership.

Norm Allen, President
Touchstone Ministries

Brian Stiller has led a full and fascinating life. His wise, experienced and practical comments are interspersed with autobiographical stories, which not only give insights into Brian Stiller as a rebuilder of broken walls, but will also surprise you with how much you learn about yourself. In learning to trace the guidance of God, this book will provoke and stimulate your thinking.

Charles Price, Senior Pastor
The Peoples Church in Toronto

Having successfully led three different types of ministries, Brian Stiller is most qualified to write a book on leadership. As with everything he does, the lessons he offers are rooted in Scripture and written with passion. A blend of story-telling and instruction, it is an insightful and stimulating read.

Bruce J. Clemenger, President
The Evangelical Fellowship of Canada

Brian Stiller's insights are powerful because they flow from a lifetime of discerning leadership in multiple contexts. If your organization is facing challenges, this book should be on your desk.

Kevin J. Jenkins, President and CEO
World Vision International

Brian is a leader of leaders. With a lifetime of effective leadership, Brian provides us with great and inspirational insights. If you are going to read only one book on leadership this year read this one.

Dr. Geoff Tunnicliffe, CEO/Secretary General
World Evangelical Alliance

When Brian Stiller speaks most everyone who knows of him listens. A proven leader for 50 years, he has pretty much "been there, done that" in national and international leadership. He is informed, experienced, insightful and inspiring. *Find a Broken Wall* encapsulates a lifetime of cutting-edge ministry.

Jim Cantelon, Author and Host of 100 Huntley Street
Crossroads Christian Communications Inc. CTS

Two people have given me courage and wisdom in leadership in defining moments of my leadership. One is Nehemiah, the other Brian Stiller, friend and mentor. They embody my definition of leadership: One who looks at their world and says, "It does not have to be this way" and does something about it.

Brian and Nehemiah have calluses and a track record to prove they are skilled leaders. Both did more than was expected, and in the face of impossible odds. They offer wisdom, down to earth common sense and experience. They both have wounds and scars of the conflict and opposition they endured. They also completed their task while staying in cadence with another's best, not just building a wall or rescuing a college, but inspiring us rather than building empires, to seeking his Kingdom. For me, I not only have a shovel and trowel in hand but now a basin and towel also.

T. John McAuley, President and CEO
Muskoka Woods

One of Canada's most inspiring faith leaders has inspired us again! Brian's story of how God called him to a life of visionary leadership and equipped him to endure its rigorous challenges is incredibly helpful to any leader intent on making a meaningful difference for God's Kingdom.

Donald E. Simmonds, CEO
Crossroads Christian Communications Inc. CTS

The most important thing in life has been Brian's passion. In this, his best book yet, he gives us life lessons on how to reach the most important. It is sage advice for leading, influencing and caring for people and projects as they come into their highest potential.

Lorna Dueck, Executive Producer, Context TV
President, Media Voice Generation

Brian Stiller is like few leaders I know—an understanding of how to lead and the gift of communication to help us understand key biblical truths and key principles. *Find a Broken Wall* uses the best of his talents and insights, surpassing most of what I've read in this area. It has something for everyone, whether a leader or member of a church. This book is the history of Brian: biblical truths he applies to the challenges he has faced and stories of what God has done under his leadership over these past decades. I highly recommend it as reading to everyone!

Hon. Jake Epp, Chairman
Ontario Power Generation Inc.

Many years ago my friend Brian Stiller drove a strategic tentpeg into the secular ground of Canada and assembled a structure where those with the same view of Christ would also find a voice in the culture. That peg was in the shadow of Canada's crumbling wall of Christian faith. He went on to give the rest of his life to restoring that wall. His legacy is that he is not just a builder, he is a re-builder. If you want to know where Brian Stiller is on any given day, go visit that wall. It is by that wall he works and by that wall he will die.

John D. Hull, President and CEO
EQUIP Leadership, Inc.

A must-read for organizational leaders, pastors, teachers and visionaries! It prioritizes encouragement, challenge and dealing with reality as a Kingdom leader. We need to multiply in increasing numbers men and women who take the challenge of building broken walls.

Geri Rodman, President
Inter-Varsity Christian Fellowship of Canada

Foreword

Find a Broken Wall is a call to action for every reader. Once each of us identifies what it is we have to offer—our God-given gifts—the next step is to listen, pay attention, and have the faith, vision, and values to go where we are needed. What is God calling you to do? It may be leading a troubled university, ministering to the needy, devoting yourself to a social cause, or even helping to fix what has broken within your own organization. With a backdrop of the Biblical story of Nehemiah, Dr. Brian Stiller challenges readers to find a place where they can make a difference—whether it be within their home town or across the globe—and then offers up the tools of effective change. This book is a gift to all of us.

Ken Blanchard, coauthor of *The One Minute Manager*®
    and *Lead Like Jesus*

Contents

Foreword 11

Introduction 15

Prologue 17

Principle 1: LISTEN FOR OPPORTUNITY IN CHAOS 23

Principle 2: RECOGNIZE OPPORTUNITY IN CHAOS 43

Principle 3: EXERCISE YOUR FAITH 65

Principle 4: DISCOVER THE VALUE PROPOSITION 83

Principle 5: BRIDGE THE DIALECTIC OF PASSION AND PLANNING 101

Principle 6: RECOGNIZE THAT RECRUITING RESOURCES IS A LITMUS TEST
            OF LEADERSHIP 117

Principle 7: RECOGNIZE THE POLITICS 135

Chapter 8: EVALUATE YOUR ACHIEVEMENT .153

Index 165

Introduction

This began with one of many conversations with friend and mentor Henry Wildeboer. He asked, "Why don't you write about what you really understand?" Without waiting for me to ask what he meant, he said, "Leadership."

So began this journey. It took a few starts. After many words in the hard drive I asked Don Loney, editor at John Wiley & Sons, to review my second draft. He had my manuscript with him when delayed at the Halifax airport, and so for those hours pored over it, and in our next time together said I was going in the wrong direction. Lifting one chapter, he focused on the Nehemiah story, giving me the title and outline. His interception was timely. For his interest and help I'm grateful.

Herb and Erna Buller were interested in this from the start, for over the years, the four of us have often sat into late evening hours, reflecting on life, telling stories and trying to decipher the ways and needs of leadership.

There are many who have contributed to my learning. In danger of missing some I want to point out those who were chairmen: Al Setter and Jim Hill, Youth for Christ in Montreal; Bruce Mathewson and Geoff Moore, Toronto YFC; Vince Walters and John Neufeld, Canadian YFC; Mel Sylvester, John Redekop, Donald Bastian, Don Jost and Ken Birch, the Evangelical Fellowship of Canada; Archie McLean, Tyndale University College & Seminary. Of course there were many in these organizations and others with whom I've worked that have had much to teach me.

Audrey Dorsch has been an editorial collegue for a number of my books. Her expertise, wisdom and editorial smarts never cease to amaze me.

One wonders what else you have to contribute to a topic that many others have written about. In reviewing the literature I saw many describe various forms and styles of leading, but none spoke about rebuilding troubled and broken organizations.

Right out of university, I learned firsthand what it takes to reconstruct a tired and out of step organization. This began a life experience of lifting and restoring ministries.

Nehemiah has been a friend of many years. Often I would read his story, looking for ideas and insights to fuel my heart, and help me see what was needed in creating new enterprises of value.

Brian C. Stiller
March, 2012

Prologue

Nehemiah wrapped his robes around him for some warmth in the cool early morning as he stepped onto the patio of his lavish apartment in Susa, capital of the Persian Empire. Last night he had been told of the impending arrival of Hanani, his brother, from Jerusalem. Bureaucratic insider gossip told him the news was troubling. But only his brother's version would he trust.

When Hanani arrived, they greeted as brothers. Their life history, friendship, and life in exile had maintained their bonds in spite of long separation. They understood each other's words, spoken and unspoken. Little chat was needed to get to the core of an issue. They also knew their roles.

While Hanani was a family man, Nehemiah had ended up in the king's court with the trusted role of senior minister to the king. The decision was not without cost: now a eunuch, Nehemiah could have neither marriage nor family. Without the prospect of descendants, his life was on a different track—his king was his life. Loyalty would not be complicated by wife or children. Sexual opportunity had no attraction. Little distracted his interest or attention—that is, until today.

Brothers embraced. As they sat on the eastern edge of the courtyard, servants brought early morning drinks and fruit. The sun pushing its way up over the horizon promised another hot day. Yet in the cool air, Nehemiah sensed another heat. There was something troubling today about his brother. Hanani's eyes hinted at a story that would soon affect Nehemiah's life.

Politics. It wasn't everything, but in Nehemiah's world everything was political. Nothing touched his world without some overplay of political intrigue.

As senior minister, he knew the goings to and forth in the court. Stories of insider manipulations came to his desk. He had eyes and ears to know what was going on, any time, any place. He was expected to know. Only Nehemiah did the king ultimately trust. He was even the last to inspect the king's food to guard against a favorite enemy ploy of poisoning.

In 586 BC, almost a century and a half before Nehemiah's time, the Babylonian King Nebuchadnezzar had overrun the Jewish community nestled on the eastern shore of the Mediterranean, destroyed the Temple and took captive craftsmen, artisans, and skilled leaders: fifty thousand to eighty thousand Jews were exiled to Babylon.

The raid occurred on a chessboard of shifting powers. Babylon (now Iraq), north and east of Israel, was in ongoing battle with Egypt to the south and west. Israel, stuck in between, was bounced back and forth, century after century, ruled by one power after another.

Cyrus, king of Persia (now Iran), took over Babylon in 539 BC without much resistance. Benevolent and tolerant, he allowed Jewish exiles to return to Jerusalem. Many Jews, led by Zerubbabel, returned and rebuilt the Temple. Other Jews, prosperous and successful where they were, saw little value in returning to their homeland.

In 529 BC Cyrus was killed and internal fighting broke out over who would be king. Eventually (519 BC) Darius took over the vast Persian Empire, which stretched from India across into North Africa. A brilliant governor, Darius organized the empire with regional leaders and by taxation built up central wealth and power.

When he died, his son Xerxes took over but lacked his father's skills in organization and leadership, and soon the empire began its long slide. The only bright spot in Xerxes' career was when he gave in to the pleas of Queen Esther to save the Jewish exiles.

In 465 BC Artaxerxes came to the throne, desperate to keep the kingdom intact. With Egypt on the cusp of rebellion, the king had to play his cards right to keep the outer edges of his kingdom—in this case Judah—from slipping into the hands of the Egyptians. Artaxerxes sent Ezra to Jerusalem to modernize the language and document the events of the city.

Then to add to Artaxerxes' woes, the Athenians in 460 BC cast their lot with the Egyptians. Not only was the Persian king faced with Athens and

Egypt ganging up on him, one of his generals, Megabyzus, turned on him (449 BC). The king was fighting battles without and within.

Jerusalem was strategic. Through it ran a primary trade route from the Tigris and Euphrates valley to Egypt. Whoever controlled Jerusalem had economic dominance.

Now Nehemiah heard devastating news from his brother: the walls of his beloved city were lying in disrepair.

Hanani's face, creased with years in the desert sun, was shadowed by sorrow. Waiting until the servants slipped away, Hanani slowly began, choosing his words carefully. Hanani, close in age to his older brother and possessing the same faith in the God of their patriarchs, knew Nehemiah had issues and concerns far beyond his own. He had no wish to encumber Nehemiah with an increased burden. But to whom could he turn? Wrestling with whether to tell him, Hanani concluded his brother would not forgive him if he was kept out of the most critical issue their people had faced in their years of exile in the Persian world.

"Brother, the news I have to tell you from our beloved city is not good. We live in ridicule and abuse. Jews who escaped when we were taken captive have finally come out of hiding. They live as scroungers and beggars. They scratch away at the soil, and are run off by our enemies, who try to keep our people from Shabbat worship.

"Then—and this will be hard to believe—while a few of our countrymen were quietly singing King David's songs, those half-breed Samaritans heckled them, attacking them with insults and clubs.

"I was humiliated. Not only did the Persians rob us blind and kill and carry off many of our best families, now the locals are making us look as if we are religious nothings. They've tried to take our faith; now they are showing signs of taking our city.

"Nehemiah, when we rebuilt the Temple, we could at least sacrifice and worship. Here is the critical issue and the one we must address: the walls of Jerusalem are in rubble. Even the doors have been burned to ashes. The stones that gave the city such protection are tumbled around. It's a disgrace. But more. It shows the Samaritans, our enemies, that we don't care. It's one thing for people to attack us, but if we do nothing, what message does that send?"

Nehemiah's heart seemed to stop. Nothing held his affection as did the Temple. "It began the night our ancestors left Egypt," he thought. He recalled the story.

The final warning Moses gave to Pharaoh was this: "In any house that is not sprinkled with lamb's blood tonight, the death angel will kill the oldest son of the household."

From that moment—the night Moses began leading the Israelites from Egypt—the Temple began. A slain lamb became the cornerstone of their religious ritual. In the wilderness they built the Tabernacle, and finally under King David's son Solomon the great Temple was built. It housed God. No mobile wilderness tent, Solomon's Temple was not only an architectural wonder, it was the holy place where confessed sins were forgiven and where voices co-mingled in praise and homage to the God of life.

Nehemiah's rise to influence in the Persian world had been remarkable. An immigrant's son becoming a senior official in government, living in luxury in the most powerful of nations, was a rare achievement. No longer a despised Jew, Nehemiah had class, status, and influence.

Now his world was about to change, his comfortable life upended by the news of catastrophe in Jerusalem. The city was not simply his ancestral home; it was the seat of his spiritual life, religious memory, and identity. While much had been done to reconstruct the city and Temple, what use was that when everything that had been built up was exposed to danger because the city's walls were in disrepair? Weeping was not foreign to his world, and Nehemiah let his feelings show.

In the following days, he found comfort in seclusion, fasting and praying. Time alone gave him focus and opportunity to craft a plan. As a Jew, and senior government official, Nehemiah made it his business to discern the intricate web of political entanglements. Time in prayer was not simply asking God for a way out; he was giving his mind to seeing what kind of plan would work. In his early years as king, Artaxerxes had been hard on the Jews in Jerusalem, ordering that all building be stopped. Nehemiah wondered whether he could persuade the king to reverse that order. He knew the news from Jerusalem might upset the Jewish exiles in Persia, and he was confident the king would do his best to keep the Jews from unrest. It was the opportunity Nehemiah needed. He watched for the right moment to lay out his proposal.

♦ ♦ ♦

It had been four months since Nehemiah heard news of his homeland. With the king's court now back in session, it was time for Nehemiah to swing into action; mourning over his stricken city would be left for another day. Visiting satraps sat with their entourages as the king opened the session. Times were tough. Rebellion was in the air. Taxation was a festering issue in many regions. The effect of conquered regions being forced to raise enough taxes for their own needs and also deliver the levies Artaxerxes expected was crippling. Nehemiah understood. Now Egypt was prowling, sending noises of its readiness to battle Persia. Sitting in between was Judah.

This was the best card Nehemiah had to play. It wasn't a story he had made up. His loyalty to the king was too deep for that. But it was a factor, and there was no need to spell out the consequences.

The king called for Nehemiah. Nehemiah answered, following protocol and meeting the dignity of the occasion. The king noticed something was amiss. When time allowed, he took his trusted bureaucrat aside.

"Nehemiah," he asked quietly, "what's wrong? My goodness, you look like you've haven't slept for days."

"With permission, Your Majesty, at the end of today's session, might I have a word with you?"

It was agreed.

And so began the remarkable journey of Nehemiah as he requested of the Persian king permission to leave his high position in Persia and return to Jerusalem to make his home city safe from those who sought its demise. This was no small request, for by such authority he affected the political dynamics of the ever-explosive Middle East. For the next twelve years, he led a ragtag group that was underfunded, underarmed, and under attack, nationalists who had a will to recreate in the city of David what any Jews worth their salt would give their eyeteeth for: protection of the very building in which Yahweh lived, the Temple.

PRINCIPLE 1

Listen for Opportunity in Chaos

"Our rabbi talks to God every Saturday."

"What makes you think so?"

"The rabbi told us himself."

"What if the rabbi lies?"

"Don't be ridiculous. God wouldn't talk to a liar every Saturday."

—George Jonas, *Beethoven's Mask*

People often lead because no one else is available or interested. You may not have visualized yourself as a leader, but then you saw a need, observed an opportunity, or felt a pent-up urge to do something, so you acted, which in turn drew people to the idea. With people following your lead, you became a leader.

Most of us end up doing something we never had in mind in the first place. When I graduated from the University of Toronto in 1966, I had laid out my goals and strategy. I missed on both counts. Almost thirty years later, in 1995, when I responded with a throwaway line to Geoff Moore, a businessman and member of the board of Ontario Bible College/Ontario Theological Seminary (OBC/OTS), I had no idea where it would lead. As Geoff and I stood with Billy Graham a few days before the area-wide meetings at the Toronto SkyDome (now the Rogers Centre), Geoff said, "Brian, we are having trouble at the school." I responded with, "Let me know if I can help." Little did I know my response would result in my life being taken over by a bankrupt college and seminary and immerse me in the bone-crunching task of creating a Christian university.

Who can predict the end? Life isn't a straight line from A to Z; it is a zigzag. Decisions made for less than stellar reasons can lead into a calling of significance.

◆ ◆ ◆

After completing an undergraduate degree (1966) and twelve months of floundering I had two offers: director of the Montreal chapter of Youth for Christ (YFC) and youth minister at a Montreal church. At that time Lily, was expecting our son, Murray, and our car was on its last legs. One position offered $65 a week salary and the other $55. Both were of equal interest. With no sense of clarity but highly aware of our coming needs, we chose the first.

Finding, to my surprise, that the YFC organization was in serious debt, I learned how to rebuild, developing skills that led to a series of wall-building ministries. Next was Toronto, where the local YFC had folded. Another rebuild. Then, following mentor John Teibe, I further developed the Canadian national YFC. Sixteen years later I accepted the call to build an idea and shell of an organization: the Evangelical Fellowship of Canada. And then a late evening phone call to help rebuild a financially under-the-water college and seminary.

That initial decision back in the '60s turned into what became my calling: to lead broken-down, distressed, and undeveloped ministries.

◆ ◆ ◆

From watching others and testing ideas, I discerned critical ingredients in building broken walls.

This analysis comes from overlaying the story of Nehemiah on what I've experienced.

Where does one begin?

Begin with hearing the cry—it may be soft and boisterous, understated or self-directed. Listen for tones of survival, for noises from places and people wanting to tell those who listen that survival matters.

Eileen Henderson leads the most unattractive group one might imagine. As director of Circles of Support, she works with convicted pedophiles released from prison. Hated by the world and turned away by their own families, they are today's "lepers." Understandably, citizens are frightened by what these released prisoners might perpetrate again.

When Eileen and I had earlier worked together in Youth for Christ, I noted her instinct was on high alert: when someone was in trouble she heard. Her passion to help was linked to an uncanny ability to discern, mixed with a loving and tough ability to find solutions.

Today, through the noise of public outrage when a released pedophile is allowed to live in the community, Eileen hears other sounds: a trembling heart, the muted cries of a man often having been abused as a child, frightened, unloved, hated, and forced to flee from one community to another. As soon as people learn he has found a place in their community, the crowds descend, justifiably afraid for the well-being of their children but forgetting that he must live somewhere. What ministry is more counterintuitive?

The story of Eileen raises an important question: Why does she catch sounds that others don't? Why I did I hear the call for help when Tyndale was teetering on bankruptcy and others didn't? Could it be that the reason that a person hears one voice and not another is because their ability to hear is rooted in their gifts?

LINKING LISTENING AND ABILITY

A corollary to listening: when one's imagination is caught by the importance and dimension of a need or an idea, this is matched by the capacity and ability to do something about it.

In working with people in an assortment of ministries I've noticed that what you hear is in line with what you can do. I use "hear" in this sense: I pick up messages that connect with my desire, passion and skill. We hear certain things because we have capacity and skills to respond with solutions. Implicit in this kind of hearing is a native or learned understanding of the nature of the need, rising out of a corresponding capacity to do something about it.

Listening to a pedophile's story, I would understand the person's plight— needing discipline, a place to stay, friends, and a job. Eileen, however, hears in an uncluttered way and identifies the critical solutions. Why? Because she has commensurate gifts and skills that give her authority to speak to the problem.

When I met with the survival committee of the board of Tyndale, although I didn't understand the business of education, I knew what was needed to right the ship, raise the sails, steady the rudder, and move it into quiet water. I had done it before. I knew it would be tough, but the elements and strategy needing reconstruction were evident.

Here is my point: there is a link between what we hear and what we can do.

Let me put it another way. My dreams—of what I would like to be and do—rise out of my ability. We are wired in such a way that our hopes and dreams connect to our gifts.

I'm not speaking of romantic or wishful dreams. As a boy I wanted to be a hockey star. After all, I learned to play street hockey in an alleyway between our church and the house of the parents of Detroit Red Wings' star Gordie Howe. Playing in the National Hockey League was a romantic dream. It came and went. Though I wasn't a slouch on the rink, I wasn't NHL material.

Let me note the distinction between *visions* and *dreams*. A dream catches my interest; it is fantasy fabricated of self-interests but not that which drives my life. A vision is compelling, that which absorbs my thinking and is linked to capacity.

A fawning fan of the pianist Paderewski gushed after a concert, "Sir, I'd give my life to play like that." To which Paderewski replied, "I did." It was more than a dream. It was a compelling vision grounded in his musical capacity and perfected by years of practice.

LEARNING THE ART OF LISTENING

Endemic among leaders is the tendency to not listen to what another has to say. Filled with our own interests and the importance of our task, we understandably are anxious that the world know. Such intemperance, however, engenders two subtle and self-destructing flaws.

It shuts off our listening: an active mouth distracts a listening ear. You may notice it's hard to do both well. And in not listening we fail to hear those noises of life waiting to be born. Do you know how many people have no one to hear their story? And how few have someone they respect who will take time to listen with interest and feeling?

So in not listening, we lose. The story, the idea, the opportunity is screened out by our compulsion to be heard. What may be next for us, what may very well be a voice of God's creation in need of an audience, is muted. A treasure designed to be given so we might take of its wealth and invest in a greater good is missed. We lose what our heart has yearned for, what in our most quiet moments we have longed for. There it was—if I had only listened.

Equally tragic are people who need to be heard. Their sense of being is diminished when dismissed or ignored. So as you listen, listen with your heart. Take note of what stirs you. Take heed when it recurs, coming back to you day after day. It may be of little interest at first. Indeed, your decision to engage may precede an inner love or passion.

◆ ◆ ◆

After sixteen years in Youth for Christ, I resigned. Board members and staff knew it was the right decision and so did I, even though I had no other job waiting and no definite ministry interests to explore.

There were, however, two possibilities on the horizon.

I had been serving on the board of the Evangelical Fellowship of Canada (EFC), a member of the World Evangelical Alliance (WEA). During an EFC executive meeting a month before I announced I would leave YFC, Mel Sylvester, president of the Christian and Missionary Alliance Church of Canada, asked. "Brian, isn't it time you left YFC and took up the leadership of EFC?"

I was surprised—I had not announced my resignation from YFC—and could only sputter non-committal platitudes. At coffee break, I pulled him aside. "Mel, how did you know I was leaving?"

"I didn't know," he said. "I just sense that this is right for you."

A few days later, when speaking at a spiritual emphasis week at Trinity Western University (TWU), philosophy professor Phil Wiebe asked me point blank whether I'd be interested in the role of senior minister at Christian Life Assembly (CLA). CLA was, and is, one of the largest churches in British Columbia, attended by several thousand people every week. Lily and I flew to the west coast early in the New Year. The preaching assignment was an opportunity for us and the congregation to get to know each other.

We had a remarkable weekend. I was moved by the congregation's vision and considered the position seriously. I asked for some time to come to a decision. Back in Ontario, I retreated to the vacation home of our friends George and Pauline Spaetzel in the Blue Mountains of Collingwood. I was several time and weather zones from balmy B.C.—and a few spiritual zones from certainty about our future.

I barely stirred. With only a Bible and a notepad, and fueled by a simple prayer, "Lord, guide my thoughts," I began reading, slowly a verse or chapter, all the while making notes. Toward late afternoon, I came to Nehemiah. Loving stories, I read on. I finished and then looked at what I had written:

> *Find a broken wall.*
>
> *Find a broken wall most ignore.*
>
> *Find a broken wall others ridicule.*
>
> *But whatever you do, find a broken wall."*

I called Phil Wiebe. "Phil, I can't come."

Surprised, he asked, "What are your plans?"

"I have none."

Within an hour, a long-time friend, Mervin Saunders, a Baptist minister in Edmonton, called. "Brian, I understand you are considering a church on the west coast. I'm calling to tell you how wrong that would be for you."

I told him of the call I had just made.

"I've just been speaking with Harry Faught, and he and I believe that it is time for you to take up the leadership of the Evangelical Fellowship of Canada," he responded.

"EFC?" I queried. "There is no organization, no funding. It has no significant place in our community and little credibility in the wider church, and for sure none in the political life of Canada."

The more I spoke, the more I heard myself describing a broken wall.

◆ ◆ ◆

Listen to stories of broken dreams; walk through rubble of failed plans; hear hurting hearts speak of missed opportunities; step over the pieces of fallen monuments. Instead of searching for the good places, rewarding salaries and benefits, popular communities and nice people, look for run-down, bankrupt communities in need of someone to lift and lead.

Hearing is more than listening, more than having gifts that connect to hearing. It requires honing.

The Jews asked about Jesus, "How did this man get such learning without having studied?" (John 7:15) His response was unexpected: If you do what you already know is the will of the Father, then you will come to know. Hearing is a learned discipline. The more one works at hearing, the more likely one will hear. Like any other ability, we use it or lose it.

While we suffer from media overload—as streams of passionate, need-laden stories wash over our hyper-stimulated feelings—nurturing a hearing heart helps us hear what's important.

UNDERSTANDING GIFTING

Nehemiah, hearing of his beloved city, listened, which led to doing. He was grieved to learn of Jerusalem's vulnerability. He was angered by the humiliation of his people, ridiculed and offended by their enemies. He was so moved by this frightful situation that he spoke to the king. But without inherent skills in moving from idea to reality, he would have been passionate but not much more.

Passion is an indicator that gifts are commensurate with the need. Hearing is connected to skills. I may think it's a good idea to design a sculpture to honor a person or event, but it will go nowhere, for I am not a sculptor. As much as I believe in the value of education, and while I've given part of my life to provide for a center of Christian higher education, I don't have passion to construct an educational curriculum. That's a clue that I'm not best suited to the task of teaching.

My generation was not familiar with theories on personal gifts. Learning about personal gifts was revolutionary. Pressured by colleagues to be like them, I was liberated when I clued in to an understanding that skills and gifts are commensurate with passion or calling: the ability to envision what needs doing is rooted in a capacity to do it. Driving ambitions move within circuits of abilities. What I'm not gifted to do I don't have passion for.

Desires to become are linked with gifts that enable the becoming. When someone asks, "What should I do in vocation?" I ask, "What do you like to do? What do your friends and family say you do best?" Once we establish that groundwork, I suggest that it makes sense to see God's call within the person's gifts.

The logic goes thus:

What I like to do is an indicator of what I do best.

God has gifted me.

Education, training, and experience serve to strengthen those innate gifts.

It would not be out of character for God to want me to use gifts he has given.

So identify your gifts.

◆ ◆ ◆

Profiled as a type A personality, I was not strong on self-awareness. With a focus on accomplishment, reflection wasn't high on my list. Others outshone me in school grades, hockey, and music. Though I seriously studied piano, my friend Mel Bowker was star pianist at both YFC and the Lyle Gustin Studio in Saskatoon where we studied. His unusually gifted and creative talent bypassed me.

This wasn't disconcerting. My goal was ministry. I loved church, music, summer camps, sermons, and preachers. After my last year of high school, attending our denominational college was a seamless choice. After college and another three years of university, I thought I was prepared for ministry. But what was that to be? Nothing held my attention as much as preaching.

I set out on my own. Lily and I traveled, we did music, and I preached. I was a disaster. Broke, we returned home. To pay bills I did roofing—until too many snow storms pushed me from roofs. Then I shoveled off skating rinks in the night and filled in as a substitute high school teacher during the day. Deeply disappointed that my boyhood dream was falling to pieces, I admitted this wasn't working.

What was missing? I needed discernment of gifting.

◆ ◆ ◆

Note Paul's outline of personal gifts.

> We have different gifts, according to the grace given us. If a man's gift is prophesying, let him use it in proportion to his faith. If it is serving, let him serve; if it is teaching, let him teach; if it is encouraging, let him encourage; if it is contributing to the needs of others, let him give generously; if it is leadership, let him govern diligently; if it is showing mercy, let him do it cheerfully. (Romans 12: 6–8)

This list of seven gifts, though not exhaustive, outlines seven primary motivations: what you or I find to be renewing. A gift is like a pair of well-fitting shoes: we can walk for extended periods without fatigue. When we try to serve with the wrong gift, soreness sets in—and we don't get far.

The gift	The related natural ability
Speaking	Able to speak in public or write, (e.g., minister, politician), often in a position requiring public speaking with the goal of persuasion
Serving/helping	Inclined to help and serve, often in fields of health care or hospitality
Teaching	Interested in relating knowledge so others will understand, often as a schoolteacher, professor, instructor
Encouraging/ motivating	Loving to support and motivate others—a gift required in positions in which encouraging others is key: management and HR

Giving	Able to give, often as entrepreneur or businessperson who can generate funds out of wise investing and management
Leading	Able to gather, inspire, and organize people toward a goal
Showing mercy	Having an instinct for people's needs, suited for work that requires empathy and wisdom in finding solutions

Figuring out your ministry includes finding what best matches your natural gifts. I played fullback in high school football. Short and stocky, I wasn't suited for the long throws or end runs as much as I was for running up and over the defense. My football nickname, appropriately, was "the bull."

In time I learned that, as much as I loved public speaking, my primary strength was not in preaching but in leading. I finally admitted it and was set free from expectations of others and especially myself.

Analyze Paul's outline and you will see the pattern of key motivational strengths.

Let's work with some models.

◆ A pastor with a combination of the teaching and mercy gifts will tend to find teaching and counseling as the base of ministry.

◆ If you are strong in leading and giving, it may suggest you have the capacity to lead a parachurch ministry or manage a multi-ministry church.

◆ A visionary with high ideals and grandiose plans but little interest or skills in sitting quietly and listening to needs may be just the person to take a moribund church, agency, or business and push it into a new plan and strategy.

Each of us, from time to time, is called on to operate in each gift. Even though my prime gift is not "showing mercy," there are situations in which I'm called on to counsel, to help a person through a stressful situation. Also, though my prime gift is not giving, I am called on to give and to do so with joy.

The point is not to be trapped into allowing a personality test or gifting chart to be the final guide. It is to serve as conversation and in a growing understanding of oneself.

To help us to see where we fit into life ministry, I've organized roles of ministry into five basic categories: pastor/minister, evangelist/apologist, educator, advocate, and leader. These are not mutually exclusive. A pastor may have leadership gifts. A person with a heart for social justice may also be a pastor, evangelist, leader, or teacher. This list asks you to identify which area most naturally suits you.

Pastor/Minister

◆ has passion to shepherd a congregation

◆ will counsel and nurture

◆ coaches, encourages

◆ teaches

Teacher/Educator

◆ loves to make ideas understood

◆ pursues scholarship

◆ teaches

◆ writes

Advocate

◆ has a concern for justice

◆ serves

◆ seeks transformation

◆ represents

Counselor

◆ has intuition for people's feelings

◆ is patient

- listens well

- builds trust

Apologist

- exhibits spiritual readiness

- loves to tell the story of faith

- represents the gospel

- is missional

Leader

- has joy in casting a vision

- is strong in team building

- instinctively networks

- sees the need to build resources

IDENTIFYING GOD'S CALLING

Linked into gifts is calling. The Spirit is ever moving and shifting us about to meet his agenda. Respecting our gifts, he moves before us and in times of opportunity helps us hear what is best—best for Kingdom purposes. In the end, what we do becomes his call.

Critical to hearing is a conviction of God's providential leading; he combines what we do best with what needs doing here and now.

In listening, Nehemiah knew it was now or never. The message delivered by his trustworthy brother allowed no mistaking of need. He also had capacity.

◆ ◆ ◆

Few people have influenced my life as my brother David. In a previous book I describe the impact that the death of his beautiful eighteen-year-old daughter, Jill, had on our entire family.

From his boyhood experience in meeting Bob Pierce, founder of World Vision, Dave discovered he had a love for the poor. Successful in business, unrelenting in keeping people accountable, and operating with an unusually high work ethic and standards of integrity, he also had a heart that reached out to the poor, regardless of the cause of their poverty.

Following Jill's death he sold his business and gave his life, leadership, and experience to organizations helping the poor. As chair of Opportunity International, his life focused on providing microloans to men and women, especially in the majority world, lifting them into sustaining enterprise, helping them find freedom and justice.

I asked him, "What was the compelling part of that life change?"

During the four years prior to Jill's death I had made numerous visits to West Africa and Asia. I had walked in very poor places, and the pictures of those hopeless slums would not let me go.

Six months after Jill died, I returned to Mali as a volunteer to evaluate a project of ninety-six wells that had just been completed in the Dogon tribe area. The drive from the capital, Bamako, took a full day, and when we arrived in the evening, it was dark. We pulled into the work compound, and as I got out of the Land Cruiser, I was faced by seven Dogon men who stepped out of the shadows and stood in front of me. The Dogon greeting can last for many minutes as they enquire about family and life. Not being able to speak my language, instead they each moved to me, gently put their arms around me and rocked from side to side, moaning and in non-verbal ways, expressing their sorrow and solidarity with me. They had heard the story of Jill's passing since my last visit. As this was happening, I remembered the statistics. These men represented families who had buried, on average, one out of every four children before the age of five. They knew this pain, and they reached out and drew me into their fraternity. Pictures of places were replaced by living brothers. Any misapprehension, that those living in difficult circumstances somehow might hurt less in the specific because their lives were filled with so many trials, melted away. Their pain was no less than mine.

That day my calling had a face, many faces. It was personal in its focus, and whatever I did had to speak directly into the hopeless situation in which the brothers and sisters of my fraternity find themselves. It must be hopeful. It must personally provide them a hand up and bring strength to the family.

As it turned out, the next twenty years of our lives were given to microcredit programs in the developing world. The stories of economic and social redemption, borrower by borrower, are many. Children from these desperately poor homes finishing school, some gaining degrees from university; medical treatment being accessible for sick children; new roofs and floors being installed in shacks to protect from the elements are only a few of the outcomes of the work that are told many times over. Christ's love for the poor was the driving force, and as we reached out in his love, transformation was a constant companion. Although my work took me into governance at the international level, it was my fraternity that gave me roots and gave me purpose.

It took a listening heart and discerning mind tuned to those he cared for, linked to his gifts of organization and leadership. Hearing and doing are joined at the hip. What compels me suggests I am able to do something about it.

◆ ◆ ◆

TRAINING ONESELF TO HEAR

What does it mean to listen?

1. Decipher the real story behind the emotion.

2. Envision what needs doing.

3. Connect the need with your capacity.

4. See that it can be done.

5. Discern that, difficult as it may be, it is possible.

It requires effort to hear. Inundated by a relentless cacophony—music; solicitations to make more money, to have more fun, to be sexier; or the ever-present newscasts of a frightening or vacillating nature—we are ever hearing of the now.

How then can we hear the deeper and less pervasive sounds of the universe? When I am brought face to face with reminders of an exploding catastrophe in sub-Saharan Africa or the devastating impact of an earthquake or tsunami, am I in danger of becoming heart-dead over these unimaginable disasters and the encroaching needs? I think yes.

Along the rough roads of leadership, God is in the moment. Our predicament may be of our doing. But failure in moral judgment or lack of insight to solve an issue is not the end of life.

Leaders, take a cue from your dreams—that which fills your mind with creative excitement. Reflect on your hopes and wishes. God is in that. It is more than psychological hype. He works out of our motivation, a clue to his gifting. It is an essential ingredient of a healthy self, the basis on which we dream our dreams. Kingdom leadership partners with God in transforming life, engaging a hurting and dysfunctional world in the power of his Spirit. We aren't selling another product or service. We are leading ministry whose mission is introducing people to eternal well-being. That takes a dream proportional to the task. Don't despise dreams. That's the stuff of God.

◆ ◆ ◆

In my midtwenties I met Jay Kessler, president of Youth for Christ U.S.A., and was intrigued by his uncanny ability to listen beneath the noise waves of a radical culture brewing in the 1960s and coming to full bloom in the 1970s. He deciphered the mood and concerns of his generation, providing us with back-door thinking. While most people peered into the world from the front door, Kessler looked for the not-so-obvious. He listened.

King David, in rebuilding Israel, chose a number of groups for reconstruction of that national enterprise. One group caught my attention. The sons of Issachar "understood the times and knew what Israel should do"(1 Chron. 12:32).

I learned from them. I began to read, listen, write, and speak with an ear to the times, to the noise of my generation. Struggling to make sense of the conflicting ebb and flow of ideas I met Francis Schaeffer, a philosopher and evangelist. He taught me how to listen in new ways. Caught in the old super-spiritual paradigm that the world was evil and the only way to live was to wait to be rescued by Christ's Second Coming, I had unconsciously disparaged the immediate world as being of little value. Only the future mattered.

Schaeffer helped set the stage for the wider world. The radical ideas of the 1960s had emerged from thinkers a generation earlier. The world of art had its own underscoring rationale, providing my generation with ideas on how to think and metaphors on what was valued.

He enlarged my capacity to listen as I came to see that all of life is the Lord's: "The earth is the LORD's, and everything in it" (Psalm 24:1). His logic was clear: if all of this creation is God's, then those of us in leadership need to take seriously the mandate of "running creation."

As I listened, what I had ignored now mattered: Great music and architecture, caring for the planet, understanding culture, crafting public policy, human rights. These and a whole host of issues, instead of being shoved outside of our mandate, mattered. I continued to have passion to tell the world of Jesus' love but that was now posited within a wider world.

It was this new kind of listening that helped me understand the importance of helping people of faith to see that if public issues matter to the Father, they should matter to us. This new worldview led in time to expanding a college into a university, shaping minds, building scholarship, and preparing leaders.

In the spring of 1995, I co-chaired, with Anglican Bishop Blackwell, the Billy Graham meetings at the SkyDome in Toronto, and was fortunate to spend time with the legendary evangelist. I watched him loving, serving, speaking prophetically, and calling our world to faith. Crowds the size never seen packed the stadium, with tens of thousands turned away.

Then, just days after his visit a phone call changed my world. Rev. Dave Collins, vice chair of the board of governors of OBC/OTS, (now Tyndale University College & Seminary), following up on my earlier conversation with Geoff Moore, said they needed a president, and needed one fast.

"I'm not interested in the job, but how can I help?" I asked.

"We need a president," he insisted.

I repeated what I had just said, and he repeated his statement. I gathered the salient facts: the schools were in serious debt, with no credit and banks refusing any further help. The entire faculty and staff—with the exception of one lonely security person—had been laid off ten days earlier.

Bankruptcy was in the offing. Unless it was staved off, there was little chance for the schools to see another academic year.

I had immediate misgivings. I was aware of the institution's influence in preparing leaders for church and missional service, in Canada and around the world. But I also knew evangelicals had a history of lacking enthusiasm for supporting Christian education. Was this my new call?

That fateful telephone conversation was Monday, June 26, the day the schools learned they had been granted bankruptcy protection. I asked for thirty-six hours to decide. I consulted Dr. Ken Birch, EFC's chair, and invited three senior staff from the college and seminary—Lynn Smith, Ward Gasque, and John Franklin—for dinner. "Don't tell me the problems, but share with me your vision," I invited.

The summer weeks of 1995 on campus were a blur. I arrived on June 28, looking at the opening of the fall semester 60 days away. The bank would extend no more credit. We had to raise enough to get the schools running by the end of August and a cushion in the account to see us through the early days of the fall.

I wrestled with logic for my involvement. Though there was an adrenaline rush in leading the rescue, many issues and tasks were outside my interest and expertise. However, I knew that a crisis creates opportunities. Having attended a Bible college in my first post-high school days, I knew it to be a boot camp for people preparing for full-time church or parachurch ministry.

But the world had changed. Seminaries were becoming the primary place for preparing pastors and missional leaders. What then, would be the ongoing role of the undergraduate college?

Our son, Murray, had graduated from Trinity Western University, a Christian liberal arts university. We had seen its impact on his life. Though he had been raised and trained in a strong church and a Christian home, his undergraduate years of learning to think as a Christian prepared him for his calling in the world of film making. I saw the importance of providing young people with a place to get a first-rate degree within a Christian worldview.

A vision began to solidify. It made sense that to build such a place in the most populous region of Canada was worth my energy and focus. I was

*not inspired to rescue an institution more than a century old. Giving my
life to keep a relic on its wobbly legs was not to my liking. However, seeing something wider and linked to the needs of our world—now that could
excite me. And it did.*

◆ ◆ ◆

FINDING YOUR WALL

How does one make choices? I have no formula: many factors influence
our decisions. Identify the essential elements that weave an emotional and
spiritual infrastructure that gives strength so you can lead with emotion,
joy, and clarity. Here are a few from my repertoire.

THAT I HAVE PASSION FOR IT

Passion is a barometer, indicating that I'm gifted to do what needs doing
and seems right to do. Without passion I'm useless. If our lives are listless,
feet shuffling with boredom of doing a task day after day, weeks dragging
by in wait of the weekend or a holiday, we become a weight on the organization. While feelings run through cycles, and there are times when we
struggle, if the actual vocation or location is not fueled by an inner drive
to accomplish and get something done, then consider getting out, and getting out fast.

THAT I HAD A MOMENT WHEN I KNEW GOD WAS
CALLING ME FOR THIS

Ask people how they came to their place and you discover there is often a
moment or word that gave confirmation of a call. It is not surprising that
Christians have stories behind which is a belief that the Spirit guided and
directed.

We come to decisions in various ways. The more cerebral may see logical
conclusions, while others, more mystical in personality and theology, may
see more direct points of God's intervention. However, if you don't have
an internal conviction that where you are matters, the tough times will be
more difficult. Biblical stories have been critical in my decision making. I
am grateful that while riding some rough patches during the Tyndale presidency I could recall a drive with Lily on Alligator Alley in south Florida
when she recounted my vocational history. I heard—in my mind—the

Spirit saying, "Brian, you've built the EFC as much as you need to. Now I have something else for you to rebuild." That was important, for as much as at times I wanted to resign, that earlier "call" had not been lifted.

THAT OPPORTUNITIES ARE REFINED WITH CAREFUL DISCUSSION

Appointments don't come out of thin air. Implicit in serving is that we are not alone, we don't serve ourselves, and we don't end up in successful service without having our calling reviewed by those we trust.

After eleven years with the EFC, I was asked if I would consider serving as president of the National Association of Evangelicals in the United States. It excited me. I was somewhat bored by the Canadian scene, so taking on the U.S. was a challenge. But Lily and I could not discern whether that was for us. Four candidates were asked to meet separately with the search committee in Chicago. Before I went, I arranged for seven friends to meet at our home the day after the Chicago meeting. Some were aghast that I would consider leaving Canada for the U.S. as they felt there was already too much of a drain of Canadian leadership to the U.S. I called Dr. Donald Reimer, who reminded me that in leaving Canada I would lose the banks of connections built up over thirty-three years and would have to not only develop new networks but learn the religious system and the political dynamics of a large and complicated country. Others thought it was a great opportunity. However, Lily and I saw this: there was no confirmation of what to do. And without that we decided to stay put. Seven months later Tyndale slipped into receivership, an opportunity we would have missed. Conflicting opinions were used by the Spirit to hold us.

THAT THE CALLING FITS WITH MY PRIMARY GIFTS

From time to time friends in struggling marriages ask if I will help. And I will, but only for a time. Most need someone gifted and trained in that area. I'm simply not able to help beyond some encouraging words. So it is with your prime calling. There are times you may be called on to fix something because it needs doing and you're closest. The trick is to locate your main vocational responsibility within your gifts. Try running a marathon in athletic shoes that are too small or too large. Blistered feet and aching joints result. To use your gifts is to walk in a calling that fits you.

THAT THERE IS A REASONABLE POSSIBILITY THAT GOALS CAN BE REACHED

At least you see it that way. Some may reason that the prize is beyond reasonable expectation. The point is that whatever is the goal, it has sufficient short-term objectives that allow you to build momentum: that what you are doing can and will be accomplished.

THAT RESOURCES CAN BE ACCESSED TO ACCOMPLISH THE GOALS

What one calls impossible another sees as a challenge. Get a fix on where resources are accessible. Launching a vision without having in mind where the essential resources can be sourced is a sure plan for failure.

THAT THERE IS A GROUP, A CELL, AND A FEW WHO WILL MAKE IT THEIR PRIORITY

Often we begin alone with an idea. The idea needs friends. Before a launch, recruit those who will make accomplishing the goal a top priority. As we built towards the purchase of a new Tyndale campus we needed a few to put this project at the top of their priorities. Two said they would give five million dollars; a few more invested three million; and others came in at two million and one million. By so doing, they signaled to others that this was a serious priority, an encouragement for others to do the same.

Learn to appreciate the connection between what catches your attention and what you are gifted to do. For it is out of our hearing that we can discern the calling.

PRINCIPLE 2

Recognize Opportunity in Chaos

Confidence and optimism are essential. It is not faking it. It's remaining optimistic through the trying times, even when it looks pretty dark. Think about Nelson Mandela. Twenty-seven years of prison. I have to imagine he got a little discouraged, but from all accounts, he never wavered in his confidence that one day South Africa would be a multiracial democracy. I am sure a few Africa Nation Congress people in prison with him said, "Nelson, you're full of it. This is ridiculous. Your optimism is misplaced here."

—Michael Useem, *Fast Company*

Tell me what you hope for and I will tell you who you are.

—Jurgen Moltmann, German theologian

Vision is the art of seeing things invisible.

—Jonathan Swift

Hearing listens. Seeing takes in the possible. Hearing identifies ability. Seeing sees the here, the now, and beyond into the "what ifs." Vision breaks us out from seeing what is expected, moving us from *what is* to *what may be.*

In *Visioneering: God's Blueprint for Developing and Maintaining Personal Vision*, Andy Stanley quoted Benjamin Zander, conductor of the Boston Philharmonic Orchestra. It struck a chord with me:

Goals can be engaging—when you win. But a vision is more powerful than a goal. A vision is enlivening, it's spirit-giving. It's the guiding force behind all great human endeavors. Vision is about shared energy, a sense of awe, a sense of possibility.

In Principle #1 I briefly discussed the difference between *vision* and *dreams*. Let me explore that a little further.

A dream is often fantasy, a fabrication of self-interest and wishes, driven by mixed motivations—altruistic, romantic, materialistic. A dream is like a cut flower—it blooms for a moment, then wilts and dies.

Vision captures and drives life; it is rooted in the soil of ongoing life. It may include fantasy. It may lead one to dabble in unrealistic plans. But it takes hold of lives, ambitions, resources, and energies. A vision is like a garden bulb—with careful planting, and given time, it grows and blooms.

Visions make a difference. What would the world be like if British parliamentarian William Wilberforce had not devoted his life to bringing down the slave trade? The son of a wealthy family, Wilberforce had everything to gain by walking away from the issue and enjoying the fruits of his inheritance. Instead, he saw the issue as cruel and as something he could help fix. It became a life-demanding vision. How many more thousands would have lost their lives in this brutal and inhumane practice—a practice critical to the economic structure of the British Empire in the eighteenth century—if he had said no to the vision? For years his motions were repeatedly defeated by the British Parliament. Finally, just days before he died, the bill passed, and slavery was declared illegal.

Would Canada even exist as a nation if Sir John A. Macdonald, Canada's first prime minister, hadn't faced down widespread opposition to build a trans-Canadian railroad? Understanding it was a daunting task across formidable territory, Macdonald also knew this massive land would never become a nation until linked east to west.

Would the worldwide growth of Christian evangelism in the last half of the twentieth century have been as strong without the vision of a Toronto pastor? In 1948, Oswald J. Smith, from The Peoples Church, spoke to young leaders at a conference in Beatenburg, Switzerland. World War II was over; Europe was devastated, both economically and spiritually; and tens of thousands of young men and women were returning home, hardened by horrors and the stress of war. Would the gospel have anything to say to them in rebuilding the world?

The young visionaries attending the conference would soon spread out across the world, passionate and driven, to meet the needs of a new generation. Those who attended included some who would go on to make notable contributions: Billy Graham, evangelist; Bob Pierce, founder of World Vision; Bob Evans, founder of Greater Europe Mission; Dawson Trottman, founder of the Navigators; Bill Bright, founder of Campus Crusade for Christ; Harold Ockenga, founder of Gordon-Conwell Theological Seminary.

In meeting after meeting, Smith asked this troubling question: "Why should anyone hear the gospel twice before everyone has heard it once?" This simple, overarching call, a heartfelt vision birthed in the life of a missionary pastor, became the rallying cry of a new generation.

As Nehemiah listened to his brother unravel the tragic story of his homeland, he discerned what disaster faced his ancestral city and jewel of the region, Jerusalem. Why did that concern him? His obligations, surely, were to his present home. Sometimes there is no logical reason why a vision captures a person at a particular moment. We are driven by complex factors: family and genes, peers and society. But we are also inhabited by the Spirit. When a moment of surprise comes and your heart is "strangely moved," take note.

Nehemiah did. And returned to Jerusalem.

WHAT IS VISION?

Vision stirs your passion, creating interest and concern, generating feelings or thoughts that emerge in your consciousness at unlikely moments.

VISION IS A NATURAL GIFT

The human personality remarkably links passion to natural abilities. Vision flows from our natural gifts: we envision what we can do.

That was true of Nehemiah. Being a cupbearer to the king was not like being a waiter. Kings under threat had to be careful, as servants or cooks were often bribed to poison them. The cupbearer guarded against this, even tasting the king's wine and food. Only the most trustworthy was chosen as cupbearer, often becoming a king's confidante. Nehemiah's status and influence rose with his ability and skill, giving him opportunity and influence to ask for the king's help.

Though vision is a gift, it is also cultivated. Envisioning is an attitude that inclines one to defer to vision in shaping conversations and plans. It is a way of life. Visionaries don't all of a sudden have a vision. It is an art, a craft, needing to be nurtured.

VISION IS SERVICE

Vision catches our attention, calling us to give our lives in service. Protecting the Jews' center of worship was a big enough challenge to draw Nehemiah away from comfort and prestige.

In Westminster Abbey you'll see on William Wilberforce's tomb this epitaph:

> In an age and country fertile in great and good men,
>
> He was among the foremost of those
>
> who fixed the character of their times;
>
> because to high and various talents,
>
> to warm benevolence and to universal candour,
>
> he added the abiding eloquence of a Christian life.

On July 26, 1833, shortly before Wilberforce died, the British House of Commons passed the bill abolishing slavery, the bill he had given his life to.

Why was he *among the foremost of those who fixed the character of their times?* He "fixed" the character of his times by vision. His eloquence enabled him to humor, cajole, and pressure fellow MPs to consider the issue. Without vision, his eloquence might have been used for other good and honorable causes, but none likely as world changing as abolishing slavery.

The apostle Paul described King David this way: "For when David had served God's purpose in his own generation, he fell asleep" (Acts 13:36). David's leadership was rooted in his generation. Surely some of his accomplishments would affect future generations of the Jewish tribes, but his vision was devoted to his people, in his time.

VISION RISES FROM WITHIN

Leaders are not so much zapped by vision from outside as they receive it from within—through ideas, feelings, observations, and instinct. I become aware of vision in a particular way: feeling excitement. I want to start planning, asking people to test the validity of an idea and inspiring others to help construct a plan and implement the process.

In my early days with the EFC, I wrestled with the nature of Christian faith and its place within government and public life. Little material was available so I wrote my own, designed to help me explain to our evangelical community what it means to be an evangelical and what the Scriptures call us to as public witnesses. I tested the material and found it resonated with leaders—members of Parliament, historians, political scientists, pastors, and business and professional lay people. Out of that emerging vision, came the Understanding Our Times seminar, given in some 200 Canadian communities, which in time became the basis for developing a national membership and eventually a funding foundation for the mission.

VISION IS DEVELOPED

Vision may come as an epiphany or word spoken as God breaks through the clutter of your search, providing insight or a compelling idea. It may take months or years of incubation. The first generation will go through many modifications over days, months, or years, influenced by conversations, articles, and books as it matures.

An idea is a thesis, a proposal, a concept that has shape, design, meaning, subject and predicate. Its substance allows one to think about it, argue, debate, pulling it that way and this.

Lily and I sat with Jim and Kathy Cantelon over dinner. He told us of their idea.

He had had a successful career: television broadcaster, pastor, and author. After raising their three children, Jim and Kathy were about to take a careening turn in their life. While serving as a senior pastor in British Columbia, Jim had been invited to speak at a ministers' conference in South Africa. One evening, while they were watching the evening news, they learned of the devastating impact that HIV/AIDS was having on families and communities of Africa. The pictures and stories were so riveting that Jim and Kathy decided to devote themselves to building advocacy and awareness, especially among church leaders. He had known about HIV/AIDS. But that evening in the South African hotel room it became personal. He felt inner passion, determination, and drive to do something about it.

When he told us of their vision he asked, "Could this be the next major stage of Christian witness and mission?" I doubted. I asked questions. I posited that, as important as this might be, I couldn't see it being epochal to the Christian mission.

How wrong I was.

The point is that in time their idea broadened and grew, focusing on justice, caring for widows and orphans. It took time for it to settle and find a coherent place within their abilities. Vision takes time to grow, to develop.

Along with the internal maturation of a vision, ongoing and changing realities alter the landscape on which our ideas are sketched. Life, in its constant change, will be different when our ideas find themselves in reality. Communities of activists flowed into Africa with medicines and education as funding from the West and Europe streamed in. As Jim and Kathy developed contacts and built bridges into Africa, they learned that the most common community had been missed: the church. As NGOs and humanitarian agencies established contacts and set up services, congregations that numbered in the thousands simply hadn't been given a look. In time, their focus on catalyzing local churches to serve widows and orphans became the means for their vision. It had found its place.

As an idea matures, as the environment changes, so do we. Earlier motivations, which may have had more to do with a desire to strike it successful somewhere, are squeezed into a heart that is now more driven by the needs of those our vision will serve.

VISION IS BORN OF PAIN

Vision can also rise from heartache and sorrow, the ashes of humiliation of personal failure, or the heartlessness of others. It may come from natural disaster or human-manufactured war. It may be born out of organizational debacle, personal insecurity, the fire of oppression and persecution, or long and lonely nights of personal travail. It comes from as many places as we live, and from as many places as our hearts find a resting spot.

Norm Allen was unceremoniously moved out of leadership in a national youth ministry. In my work with leadership staff, I had never seen anyone who had such peer influence. Amid the normal uprooting one feels in such a vocational disruption, Norm, rather than dwelling on his misfortune, instinctively turned to his gifts: influencing people toward faith. He had worked for years on high school campuses; those high school students, now mature and involved in business and leadership, needed a mentor and spiritual guide. Touchstone Ministries became the framework for providing spiritual growth for those who found much of the formal church to be less than helpful.

VISION IS CREATED IN CHAOS

Visions are often born out of crisis. The news of Jerusalem's vulnerability was sufficiently sad that Nehemiah listened. C.S. Lewis reminds us that suffering is God's megaphone to a broken world. Often we simply miss the story because life is going fine. But catastrophe presses us to listen.

If Tyndale had not been in meltdown, would it have attracted my attention? When asked to help, I asked historian Dr. George Rawlyk of Queen's University what the loss of Tyndale would mean to the evangelical community in Canada. He said there was nothing else in Canadian church history that could match such potential loss. That got my attention.

Visions aren't isolated realities cut off from others or issues. Nehemiah wasn't building a wall. He was protecting Jerusalem. More, he was restoring the witness of the people of God.

◆ ◆ ◆

Let me tell you of a moment when I learned about vision's potential impact.

The birth of a vision to change an undergraduate Bible college into a full university came during a private conversation with board chair Archie McLean. The seminary was well designed and suited to carry on the training of pastors, missionaries, and church leaders—tasks that had been the purview of the Bible colleges for many generations—and it had served our Canadian community well. It seemed to us that the college now should become a place where young people would receive strong and vibrant academic training in a Christian setting, demonstrating the wisdom and presence of God in the totality of life.

The world had changed since my years at the University of Toronto in the 1960s. High school graduates, after twelve years in a secular environment, usually haven't experienced the integration of faith and learning. Too many end up in educational experiences where what they believe and what is taught segments their lives. Even a student nurtured in faith at home, church, and summer camp may be ill prepared to face a professor debunking faith or taking pains to show how religious faith is out of sync with postmodern learning. What intellectual strength does a nineteen-year-old first-year student have to combat the well-rehearsed lines and logic of a teacher armed with a PhD and a lifetime of argumentation? It's not unlike dropping a child off on a major highway and telling him to cross alone.

To meet this challenge, our community needed a change. More than that, we needed the provincial government to permit a non-government-supported school to become a university. That became the seed that grew into the only Christian university in Toronto.

Seeing what might be was critical in moving a bankrupt college and seminary into a new century and mission.

The next hurdle was property and facilities. But that for later.

◆ ◆ ◆

Vision stirs us to do something. It connects to our natural gifts, taking hold of our attention with a heart to serve others. Though outside influences affect the way we see life, vision bubbles from within, triggered by a word, experience, newscast, personal tragedy, humility or sorrow, a picture, or for me, stories from the Bible.

As hard as it may be to pinpoint how vision surfaces in life, we can see what vision will do—for ourselves as individuals, for those we work with, and for the project or mission at hand.

WHAT DOES VISION DO?

VISION LIFTS HEARTS

In the darkest moments, vision calls us to think grander and more important thoughts. Hope creates the environment in which we think and act. When people and organizations are broken and dysfunctional, they languish.

Self-doubt and other-inflicted wounds, if allowed to fester, will undermine and diminish any positive notion.

Vision stimulates the mind to rise from ashes, seeing what is possible. Vision doesn't ignore or deny reality but believes that disaster is not all there is.

You can't predict what will kindle inspiration in others. Tyndale had an unpaved parking lot, dusty in the sunshine and a mudhole in the rain. Two years after I arrived, the city informed us that they were so fed up with Tyndale not doing what we had promised—pave the parking lot—that they threatened might close us down. That created a perfect opportunity to do what had been low in our priorities. To my surprise, when we put out the word, we raised the money in days, and the paved parking lot became our symbol of renewal. People assumed that if we could get the mudhole paved we could do anything!

VISION EMPOWERS

A visitor standing at the building site of St. Peter's Basilica in Rome turned to a worker sweeping up the construction debris of the day and asked, "And what are you doing?" The sweeper replied, "Building a great temple for God."

There was brilliance somewhere in that community of workers. Some manager was smart enough to draw everyone, from Michelangelo to the sweeper, into the vision of the task.

Ministry is done amid the grind of daily tasks. The challenge of leadership is to lift the eyes of our colleagues so that in building, they see their tasks as being more than sweepers. A compelling vision gives heart and drive to all, be they staff, donors, or friends, creating a conviction that something can be done. In turn the vision becomes theirs as they tell stories of the vision to others.

VISION GIVES PURPOSE TO OUR WORK

Secure though I was in my call to Tyndale, I became what I had never wanted to be: an administrator. When I left the EFC, a friend described how I felt: "Brian, as a Canadian leader you have moved from being conductor to first violinist."

FIND A BROKEN WALL

I had stepped from the national stage of debating issues, of meeting with political, social, and religious leaders, to running a nine-acre property. I had moved from engaging on the major matters of the day to managing schools. My world had shrunk. My sense of meaning to the national church diminished. Yet I never doubted I was where I had been called to serve.

Bill Hybels, pastor of Willow Creek Community Church in Chicago, viewed situations such as I was in this way: "Subordinate your own life's agenda in order to carry out the vision he has given you."

For purpose to rule, personal subordination is required. What do you do when what you feel you are called to do cuts across your life's agenda? You work at consciously setting aside what matters to you personally. It is good to live to a higher purpose than your own. Soldiers do it. We can too.

VISION MOTIVATES OTHERS

Vision does what nothing else can do: lift people into a zone of enthusiasm and personal commitment. As Nehemiah's vision became their vision, those who followed Nehemiah were empowered. In a complex world, where we get lost in the dreariness of daily living, purpose—which vision can bring—fills a person with meaning. And from that inner motivation people more enthusiastically select what is important in the use of their resources and time. Vision brings together resources, making the many together much more powerful than the many apart.

In public speaking I seek to encourage, looking for an updraft of enthusiasm to carry the audience into feelings of optimism. But those moments go quickly. Motivation that lasts has to grip one's dreams, waking moments, and priorities.

Vision can be understood by story. Frame your vision by describing what was, what is, and what will be. A story not only helps people remember the idea but gives them a framework to tell of the vision. The more they tell others the story, the more the vision will provide fuel for their own motivation.

VISION ESTABLISHES PRIORITIES

Mike Shanahan, former coach of the Denver Broncos football team, once said, "If you don't have the Vince Lombardi trophy, everything else is a paperweight."

As much as many professional football players may be hugely compensated by money and status, winning the Super Bowl sets priorities. Such a compelling vision sees players through the rough and hard moments of a bruising career.

Assembling your daily schedule around what matters will make an enormous difference. Review your schedule for the past month. How much time was given to what you really want to accomplish? We all have bits and pieces of administration that need to be done, but do you force your schedule so you have time to work on vision?

Put your vision in front of you. Make it what you first see at the beginning of the day. Diversionary claptrap—as vital as it appears to be—can push vision from first place in your schedule, and "stuff" will become your trophy, with vision demoted to being the paperweight.

More important than job descriptions and annual reviews is the importance of going back to first principles: vision. That matters more than accolades of peers or managers—to know in real time and heartfelt emotion that vision continues to call you.

We endanger our people and organizations if we don't regularly remind each other of vision.

VISION AMALGAMATES RESOURCES

Andy Stanley reminds us that "Vision forms in the hearts of those who are dissatisfied with the status quo."

As demoralized as were the ragtag Jews in Jerusalem, as soon as Nehemiah told them of his vision, they said, "Let us start rebuilding." The many tributaries of abilities and interests flowed into a single river, pulsating with drive, care, and ability. Vision has a way of doing that.

Try asking staff independently, "What is our vision?" Can each describe it with reasonable accuracy? Also attitudes, work habits, customer relations, and profitability will let you know if a common vision is gripping the organization. Before you hire consultants to sniff around the organization, look at vision.

VISION MATURES THE LEADER

Vision matures us, pushing us to consider new ideas. Over time we figure out the difference between hype and substance. I've hurt myself and others by getting excited about an idea and moving too quickly, without proper evaluation and a careful work plan. But this too is how we learn. Success never comes without failure. My youthful vision of launching a national preaching mission failed, but in making the attempt I learned better to screen ideas and find what is primary.

VISION PROVIDES FOCUS

In *The Leadership Secrets of Billy Graham*, Harold Myra quotes Fred Smith speaking of Graham's critics: "Sometimes if a racehorse pays too much attention to a horsefly, it makes the fly too important. Some people's only taste of success is the bite they take out of someone whom they perceive is doing more than they are."

Nehemiah faced a barrage of critics. Those in opposition had a lot to lose. They were fighting for their economic existence.

The sting of fair criticism smarts. Vision doesn't eliminate the hurt of criticism, but it helps us focus. There are times when we wrestle through sleepless nights, replaying tapes of our defense, edited and refined through multiple playings.

But when criticism is unfair, undeserved, or inaccurate, what then? Smith warns us not to give it more credence than it deserves. His picture is compelling: a horse coming down the last quarter mile, fussing about a fly!

VISION LINES US UP WITH WHAT ELSE IS GOING ON

Vision does focus attention, but in so doing, it can blind us to a better way. The apostle Paul and his associates set out to visit churches in Asia Minor (Turkey). But everywhere they went, "the Spirit of Jesus would not allow them to" (Acts 16:7). Paul didn't realize his plans weren't lining up with the Spirit's agenda, which was—as we now see it—to make the geo/political leap from Asia into Europe. Paul was stuck in Asia Minor, not seeing the enormous harvest field of Europe.

In a night vision Paul heard a voice from Macedonia in Europe, calling him to come and help. This brought him in line with what else was going on. Unwittingly, Paul was being influenced to bring his vision in line with a grander plan. This wasn't a modest reorganization of their plans. It was a massive leap; and from that the gospel spread through the West and the world.

WHAT DOES IT TAKE TO FULFILL A VISION?

DEFINITION

Fulfilling a vision takes more than a fuzzy dream. Nehemiah rode through the ruins of Jerusalem, calculating what the vision required. He needed firsthand knowledge of the situation. As deeply moved as he had been when his brother first told him of the dismal state of his beloved city, and as passionate as he had been in describing the predicament to his king, it was now time to define the problem and outline a solution.

Visionaries can be dangerous, blinding people to reality. Though pushing boundaries is our responsibility, a clear definition of vision presses us to be more then hyperbolic, to consider defined and testable assumptions of what it is and what is required. This is not only for ourselves. How can we recruit others to an idea so obscured by emotional overlay that they won't be able to see it clearly or have anything substantial on which to make an informed choice?

Later I will deal with the importance of crafting a vision that has viable and understandable plans attached to it.

TESTING

Give an idea time to mature; test its workability. Nehemiah didn't pray that someone else would do it; he evaluated the problem, reviewed what was needed, and tested it with those he trusted.

Eric Hoffer, a longshoreman on the California docks with next to no formal education, spoke sanity into my generation of the '60s and '70s. He saw past the arrogance of many leaders of his day and wrote in *The True Believer*, "In times of change, learners inherit the earth; while the learned find themselves beautifully equipped to deal with a world that no longer exists." The "learned"—Hoffer speaks with tongue in cheek—merely think they are.

He knew that learners learn with an attitude of humility: there is so much more for me to know.

There are two kinds of "learned" leaders, those who are insecure but want their team to believe that they know it all, and those who don't know that they don't know. The latter assume that their ideas are right, best, and doable. A powerful vision can be dangerous. If we understand that what we lead people into doing has impact for either good or bad, we will be aware of the responsibility and risks that go with it. A secure leader is willing to test an idea against a critique to examine value, timing, and resources.

That doesn't mean a leader likes the critique or agrees with it.

During my last year as president at Tyndale I worked on a proposal to launch a special study center at the seminary. The cabinet agreed to support it. The executive of the board of governors approved it in principle. I had the director and the money for the first three years.

However, I had not sufficiently tested the workability of the idea. It was eventually torpedoed.

CONFIRMATION

"Visions are born in the soul of a man or woman who is consumed with the tension between what is and what could be," comments Andy Stanley.

Seeking confirmation isn't about camouflaging insecurity. It is finding someone you trust who, with wisdom and prudence, offers support. Now and then we need someone to sit in the applause section, especially in the tough times when we wonder if the idea was crazy at best.

We live in the tension of *what is* and *what could be*. Leaders push out from the shore, refusing to sail in shallow waters. And there is the risk. We need confidants—those who will look into our eyes and, with love and care, speak words of support.

Mel and Marion Sylvester were those for me. As we rebuilt the Evangelical Fellowship of Canada, we had no money and no plan. Yet they faithfully confirmed, in my hearing and others', that they believed I was uniquely called and gifted for this role. Their love was evident, made sure by their confidence. In the first few years of start-up, I knew they believed, and for me that was enough.

HARD WORK

Doing something of value calls for personal investment: nothing good comes easily. "Shortcuts to excellence" is a misnomer. Gardener Constance Casey, in an article in *Slate* magazine, speaks of the hard work that beauty requires:

> Like a lot of beautiful things, tulips inspire malfeasance, and they take a lot of work to maintain. Careless people pick them. Mice, rats, moles, skunks, squirrels and deer eat them. Even in Holland, they need a lot of human intervention to thrive, because they'd rather be on a rocky mountainside in Turkey, where they come from.

Leading, like growing tulips, isn't easy. Leaders start out on a journey that inevitably requires a kind of death. Jesus provided an illustration: a seedling doesn't reproduce or grow unless it falls into the ground and dies—followed then by sprouts overcoming resistant soil, pushing into daylight, drawing in nutrients.

Recall the minister who stopped by a parishioner's farm. Looking over the meticulously cared for field, he commented, "Isn't God's creation beautiful?"

"Yeah, I suppose," the farmer grunted, "but you should have seen it when he had it all to himself."

The gifting of God is not automatic. We've all seen tragic failures of people who were gifted yet by poor choices, crippling life experiences, or laziness frittered away their lives, leaving the bulbs carelessly tossed aside in a corner of the garden.

Of those who have much, much is required. It will sound hollow as we enter the Kingdom and, when asked for the return on investment, mutter, "I was persecuted; I ran out of energy; I felt insecure; I couldn't make up my mind; no one would listen." Blooming calls for daily, conscious investment and labor.

Vision is not a half-baked idea that you ask God to bless; it is that which has been defined, something worthy of sacrifice. If it is half-baked, then wait. Let it first emerge as workable and saleable. Launching too soon can ruin what might otherwise be a treasure.

MORAL CONVICTION

Christians called to lead, whether in making widgets or doing Bible trans-
lation, discover convictions in biblical values. Believing they have been
called to serve, they want to be accountable for what they do and how they
do it.

A banker working outside of Canada noted that basic working assumptions
on which he had learned to operate didn't transfer. In investment banking,
he was accustomed to agreements made by a handshake, with contracts
later drawn up by the lawyers. Where he was now operating, elementary
ethics were overlooked if something else was thought to be of more value.
Built on an ethical bog, this culture had little understanding of accountability, seemingly uninterested in a framework of honesty and integrity.

VISION BEYOND ONESELF

As I viewed a Hubble image of a far-off constellation, it reminded me that
too often I live within narrow plans, oblivious to God's wider world.
Susceptible to forgetting that our life is part of a greater world, we are in
danger of speaking appropriate platitudes, operating organizational
machinery, and doing our best to predict need and resources without being
aware of the Spirit, his interests, connections, agenda, and timing.

◆ ◆ ◆

*It was the early summer of 1996 and I faced the biggest challenge of my
life. Weeks earlier I had informed Archie McLean, the newly appointed
chair of the board of governors of Tyndale, that I would come on as full-
time president.*

*One day my wife—knowing Tyndale's financial distress—pointed to the
campus of the Sisters of St. Joseph, just west of our campus: "Brian, someday the Lord will give that to you." Those fifty-six acres were arguably
among the most desirable in the city of Toronto. Located inside the north
perimeter of the city, just a few minutes' bus ride from the proposed new
subway line, this campus was the pearl of North Toronto. Framed by a
beautiful landscape, watered by the East Don River, it included what many
say is the most beautiful chapel built in Canada in the twentieth century.*

*Lily's prophetic announcement helped me see the strategic importance of
the property. Tyndale's site at the time—almost adjacent to St. Joseph's—*

was too small a campus from which to launch a Christian university. Where could we house a bachelor's degree in education? Where would we locate a school of business and other programs—media and journalism, social work, and fine arts, to name a few?

For the next nine years, as we worked our way through regulatory fields, paid off debt, and rebuilt our reputation, I continued to believe this adjoining campus would be ours. I read Hebrews 11 as a promise: "By faith Abraham, when called to go to a place he would later receive as his inheritance, obeyed and went, even though he did not know where he was going" (11:8). The word of faith Lily had spoken that afternoon was fixed in my mind, not as a good idea but as reality. The actual delivery of the promise was only a detail to fall into place some time in the future.

Sister Margaret Myatt, General Superior of the Sisters of St. Joseph, and I met, and over the following months we learned of each other's ministries and plans. Being uncharacteristically cautious, I said nothing about what I really hoped would be our new campus.

Over coffee one morning I asked Sister Sue Mosteller, a member of the Congregation of the Sisters of St. Joseph and former co-director with Henri Nouwen at Daybreak, her counsel. "Is the Holy Spirit leading you and do you believe this is the place he has reserved for Tyndale?" she asked. "Then you need to tell that to Sister Margaret. She, too, is being led by the same Spirit, and her desire is that the facilities be used for a witness to our world of Jesus Christ."

I drafted a letter to Sister Margaret and asked Sister Sue for her thoughts. Her response, "Brian, you need to tell Sister Margaret exactly what you have in mind. The letter needs to thump with vision." So I rewrote it. The letter initiated a conversation with Sister Margaret that set in motion negotiations. Eventually the congregation decided to sell. Our negotiating teams worked out an agreement, and in January 2006 we signed a letter of intent that was forwarded to the Vatican for approval.

As Sister Margaret and I had walked the quiet lanes of growing friendship, I knew I would soon face the inevitable mountain we would need to climb: raising money for the purchase. This would be unprecedented. No Christian church or organization in Canada had ever attempted to raise the close to $60 million we needed to buy the property, remodel and build facilities, and provide funds for new programs and academic chairs.

What we needed was someone known as a public leader, a Christian with a heart for first-class education, someone courageous in leading such an aggressive capital campaign. I had met Tim Hearn, president and CEO of the Imperial Oil Company of Canada. I invited him and his wife, Susan, to the school. Their daughter was attending a Christian university, so I knew Tim understood the importance of a Christian university education.

Some time later, in his office I said, "Tim, I have an idea."

I gave him a quick outline of the plans for the new property and then said, "Tim, I need someone of your stature to chair the capital campaign cabinet." Without delay he said, "Sure. I'd love to."

That began an exciting, faith-driven experience. Some doors we didn't expect to open, but open they did. Others we expected to open didn't.

When Lily pointed to the fifty-six acres of the Sisters of St. Joseph, she wasn't on her own. It was part of the "conspiracy" of the Spirit. Over the years, as alumni, donors, and leaders heard of our long-term plans for growth, they would whisper, "Brian, have you ever thought about the lovely Roman Catholic campus on Bayview?" After asking why, diffidently they'd whisper, "I've prayed for years that someday it would be Tyndale's."

Later our librarian, Hugh Rendle, showed me a copy of the college's 1977 yearbook, the first year the schools had just purchased the Regis campus from the Jesuits, a facility lying just behind that of the Sisters. In that yearbook the editor had included a photo of the Sisters of St Joseph campus. Under the picture the caption read, "This year Regis, next year???" The idea of acquiring the Sisters' campus was years old. Others had already, thought, discussed, dreamed, and prayed about it.

What was going on? The Spirit had planted the idea in the minds of many over the years. This "conspiracy" was his work. Before Mr. Morrow donated the property to the Sisters, and even as they designed the facilities, the Spirit had this in mind. Before Sister Margaret Myatt and I met and developed a friendship and then a partnership, the Spirit had his designs. In building friendship with the world-renowned writer Henri Nouwen, I became friends with his colleague Sister Sue Mosteller, a member of the Congregation of the Sisters of St Joseph, who I relied on to help me proceed. We were all the Spirit's handmaids.

60

While we were slugging our way out of debt, working with government to become a university, recruiting the faculty we needed for an outstanding university and seminary, all the while the Spirit was assembling people and resources—within his time.

◆ ◆ ◆

PASSION

Passion, a word associated with the suffering and death of Jesus, is rooted in the notion of extreme and compelling emotion: an underlying sense of something that is of supreme importance. An Olympic athlete pours years of training and discipline into a sport, with a heart to win. Everything comes second to that.

It's not that there is only one thing in which we invest passion. However, passion is both a signal as to one's gifts and a barometer of how much the vision matters. If there is little passion, or if it has diminished, be warned.

This affects everyone in the organization. If people lack passion, it is likely their work will be done poorly, take too long, lack pride, and be marginal in quality. Passion is a make-or-break factor. Raise that to leadership level and its impact is multiplied.

Skills, abilities, and energy all matter to what I do. Over some four decades of leading, I've grown in knowledge and know-how, but the hardest lesson has been that when passion is missing, 95 percent of who I am isn't there. It's as clear a test on calling as I can find.

HUMILITY

Mary Teresa Bojaxhiu at age 18 knew her life would be different. At 38, she founded the Missionaries of Charity. For another 20 years she worked in obscurity. We know her as Mother Teresa.

She died the same day Princess Diana died. A columnist noted, "Princess Di touched the poor, Mother Teresa took them home."

No one in our generation defined Christian love as she did. Mention her name, and images of care and compassion surface. What we forget is that she spent years in drudgery and obscurity before her name and work blazed across the world. The service that had its impact later was refined in years of obscurity. (That is not a promise that what we do in obscurity will inevitably find its way to a Nobel prize.)

The validation of our calling and value of our work may never surface. William Carey's forty years of missionary labor with one convert was not the measurement of his calling or effectiveness.

SACRIFICE

During the rise of Hitler and the increased oppression of the church in Germany, Dietrich Bonhoeffer, pastor and theologian, traveled to America to study. But he soon decided it was wrong. Eberhard Bethge, in *Dietrich Bonhoeffer: Eine Biographie,* quotes from a letter that Bonhoeffer wrote to his mentor and professor Reinhold Niebuhr:

> I have come to the conclusion that I made a mistake in coming to America. I must live through this difficult period in our national history with the people of Germany. I will have no right to partic-ipate in the reconstruction of Christian life in Germany after the war if I do not share the trials of this time with my people.... Christians in Germany will have to face the terrible alternative of either willing the defeat of their nation in order that Christian civ-ilization may survive or willing the victory of their nation and thereby destroying civilization. I know which of these alternatives I must choose but I cannot make that choice from security.

He returned to Germany and in 1945 was killed. His letters and papers written while in prison continue to speak to generations long after his death.

WHAT IS THE VALUE OF VISION?

Vision is a priceless treasure; care for it. Of the billions of ideas dreamed, yours or mine is but one. Does it matter? Will it make a difference? We don't know at first. In a sense it is like with children. In our hopes for our children, we can't predict what they may become. But we won't take a chance. Even though they are among billions of other humans, that they are ours means we have responsibility. We will do everything to ensure they have the best opportunities. Each one is priceless.

Vision is a great gift; don't squander it. The managing of vision depends on many factors, one of which is how we steward the vision. Do we give it sufficient time? Do we provide adequate investment of resources? Second-generation wealth too often finds itself in the hands of children who squander it. It has come too easy. They may have grown up with a sense of entitlement. Likewise if you have been blessed with a rich experience of family and faith, don't assume that will naturally lead you into successful ministry or leadership. Entitlement is not part of the biblical vocabulary. Nurture your vision. Build it carefully, knowing that what you invest in it will, in part, predict the result.

When is vision substantive and when is it transitory or diversionary? How do I know it deserves attention? Here are questions to ask as you evaluate your growing vision.

1. Is it consistent with what I've been learning?

2. Is it consistent with who I am?

3. Does it seem right?

4. Does it seem impossible or just difficult, and do I know the difference?

5. Have I given it time?

6. What do my closest advisors/friends say?

7. Is it an excuse to get out of where I am?

8. Is it something for which I have passion?

9. Can there be a trial run to test it?

Vision gives life and energy. Seeing beyond what is to what may be, fuels passion. Like a specimen in a petri dish, ideas, when nurtured, may lead to extraordinary possibilities and discoveries.

PRINCIPLE 3

Exercise Your Faith

Fear knocked.

Faith answered.

No one was there.

—Author unknown

You must at some point take a "leap of faith" toward the emerging
model of what it means to truly lead and away from the need to be
successful, famous, rich, in control, or powerful. The kind of leadership I
am advocating is out of the understanding of pain, the loss of innocence,
the love of others, the larger purpose, the pursuit of wisdom, the honor
of life. Ask yourself if you are willing to take the risk.

—J. Hagberg
Real Power: Stages of Personal Power in Organizations

FROM ATHENS TO JERUSALEM

It was the summer of 1995 as Tyndale wrestled the dragons of debt, anger
of faculty and staff, consternation of students, investigation by accrediting
bodies, and dismay of the church and donor community. With the entire
operation shut down, there were two possible answers to the question,
Will Tyndale survive?

I was new to the scene. I had been a guest speaker at Tyndale's chapel and
had dedicated its new seminary campus a few years earlier, but I knew little of its operation. So when people asked if it would survive, there was no

advantage in my offering a vague or modestly hopeful prognosis. I had to choose between Athens and Jerusalem.

These two cities are characterized by age, influence, and their ancient patriarchs of wisdom. Athens—with its theoreticians and philosophers, including Socrates and Plato, and their universal themes—is symbolic of theories, philosophy, and ideas. From those theories emerged countless ideas, from politics to mathematics. To the Athenian mind, truth was found in a proposition of logic or science, rooted in trusting the human mind.

Jerusalem—with Abraham and King David creating a history of leadership and nationhood—is symbolic of action, courage, and faith. From that world came various realities, from religious faiths to political conflict. To the Jerusalem mind, truth was found in plans, strategies, and actions, rooted in trusting the Lord of the universe.

It's a choice. We can continue to operate in our wisdom and strength, the systems and logic of our organizations and disciplines, or we can deliberately strike out on a course filled with uncertainty and ambiguity. The kind of choices we make don't tell us what we are doing day by day as much as they describe our mindset.

In the early days at Tyndale I came to relearn the third principle in building: faith.

Let's review our first two principles:

◆ Hearing connects your gift of leadership to opportunity.

◆ Envisioning articulates opportunity—to you and others.

Third: Faith actualizes opportunities, moving them to reality.

MEANING OF FAITH

We use the term *faith* loosely. Someone may ask, "What is your faith?" meaning, "What is your religion?" Or someone may say, "I have faith the Dow Jones will reach 15,000."

In its various uses, *faith* is often used interchangeably with *hope* and *belief*. That's a mistake. Faith is neither, although closely linked to both.

Hope is not faith. Hope is of the heart, an emotional construct of life and the world, the wide canvas on which we sketch our landscape. It is our paradigm or emotional context of daily life. When a friend dies, hope provides framing for death, for hope in Christ tells me the great story of the past, present, and future. In sorrow, I hope. The heart-breaking moment of saying goodbye is softened by hope that there will be a coming hello. Life is seen as a time frame beyond ours, a universe defined more broadly than our planet, and a mode of living more diverse than our molecular definitions.

The Christian hope is that life in its entirety is lived under the watchful care of the Lord of the universe and that death is not the end but the beginning of our next chapter.

Hope is an attitude, the shaping of daily existence. Hopelessness is a psychological state in which the possibility of value emerging, today or in the future, is rejected.

There are two aspects of hope: one's emotional disposition and the object of one's hope. Some people are naturally inclined to see the world as a glass half full, optimistically seeing opportunity all around. In the popular vernacular, they are hopeful.

Whether hope is wise or foolish is determined by the object of one's hope. Hope in and of itself is not necessarily good. Wrongly placed, it can be destructive. It depends on what one places one's hope in. Those who followed Jim Jones to Georgetown, Guyana, had hope, but a hope that was badly misplaced.

Belief is not hope. Belief is of the mind: what I deem to be true. It is cognitive. It may begin with or be shaped by hope, but belief is what we describe. Though believing is personal and emotional, it can be stated. In a sense, it is objective; it can be written, debated, and edited.

Faith is not hope (of the heart) or belief (of the mind) but action (of the will). Faith is what we do.

"I have faith in God" may mean many things. The person may be saying,

◆   I believe God exists.

◆   I will go to heaven because of God.

◆   I'm not an agnostic or atheist.

However, faith is something quite different from these affirmations.

As we explore faith and its central value in leading, let me first tell you how this became critical in rescuing Tyndale. When I agreed to rebuild Tyndale's broken walls, a powerful Old Testament story was pivotal in my decision, and over time it became a source of comfort and encouragement.

◆ ◆ ◆

Earlier I noted that, in processing the invitation to serve as Tyndale president, I asked three senior faculty and staff members about their vision. As we concluded our dinner meeting, Lynn Smith said, "Brian, this morning Roger and I, in our devotions, read Joshua 3."

The chapter tells the story of the new young leader, Joshua. Moses had died, and after forty years of wandering in the Sinai Peninsula, the Israelites wanted to possess the land promised. They asked Joshua, who in turn asked the Lord. His instructions were that as the priests walked into the Jordan River, the Lord would stop the water and the people could walk across on dry ground.

Then Lynn asked, "Brian, would you be our priest and walk into the water?"

Now, how could a Pentecostal minister's son from the Saskatchewan prairies turn down such a request?

This story became the metaphor that I often returned to over the coming years. My acceptance of the challenge was not based on knowing how we would get "there"; rather it was Lynn's overture that triggered in me the gift of faith.

◆ ◆ ◆

If you need a detailed job description and the promise of remuneration and sabbaticals, then rebuilding probably isn't for you. Building new ideas or rebuilding crumbling walls isn't usually accompanied by clear plans. Most likely the terrain hasn't been scouted. Roads haven't been mapped. What is probably needed is a compass.

In the grand narrative of the Jewish people, no story better describes this essential element of operating by compass than that of Abraham. His life describes faith: a powerful gift that fueled a willingness to gamble, making him father of not one but two nations.

My learning about leadership matured as I understood that faith is central to leading. I had been raised in a church world where faith was a frequent topic on preachers' calendars. As a risk taker, I assumed that leadership and faith were in cahoots, naturally linked. Even so I missed faith's operational essence.

The writer of Hebrews nuances its meaning in chapter 11. The King James Version gives it color: "Now faith is the substance of things hoped for, the evidence of things not seen."

Faith requires that what I hold in my hand be considered substantive even though it is not yet: it is what I can currently see as the coming reality. It isn't pretense, a foolish stunt to bolster belief or to prove I'm right.

Faith is also evidentiary, to use courtroom language. Faith reverses the usual pattern in which evidence proves what happened. Jurisprudence is based on evidence of what took place. Instead the biblical writer uses it to point to what is on the way.

Faith comes at it from the other side. It looks forward and offers evidence now of something coming to pass later.

Hold that thought. Now let's see how the New Testament text unfolds faith by way of historical examples in Hebrews 11. As the writer develops examples of faith, he drops in an extraordinary bit of advice: "Without faith it is impossible to please God."

Are you sure? Can't I please God by being good? By being holy and circumspect? By giving my life in service to others?

There is something about faith that pleases God. What might that be? *Faith is risking, knowing that without the help of the Lord I'll fail.*

Faith is action, counting on the Lord to be there. In the Hebrews text, those who are pointed out for their faith are chosen because of their *acts of faith*. Faith is an act of the will. It is what we choose to do. And in choosing we trust in the enablement of God.

This risk-taking choice is not foolhardiness but is based on understanding the task, the importance of the enterprise, and the need to move forward.

Faith is founded on belief. Hope provides the wider narrative. The biblical text, in its varieties and combinations, weaves a story that enables hope.

We begin each day with God's promise that he will be with us and that our lives will have meaning and purpose. We then live out the day with belief in his promises that we can live in fellowship with the creator of life. This belief is framed by hope.

While faith rests on hope and belief, it is set in motion by our will: what we chose to do, knowing we are in need of God's help to succeed. You can believe the Scriptures to be true but not act in faith. The New Testament writer James reminds us that even devils believe. Faith risks on belief.

Abraham had a construct of belief in place. When the call came, he already believed in God. His choice to move out from home—where to, he had no idea—was an act of faith based on belief.

Nehemiah knew where Jerusalem was located. He needed no road map. However, he had no assurance that, even if he got favor from the king and resources for the rebuilding, success would result. He risked, making of the king a request that set in motion a series of events ending in protecting Jerusalem.

Anne Lamott writes, "The opposite of faith is not doubt but certainty."

How counterintuitive! To have faith, shouldn't I be certain? Shouldn't people of faith be sure of what they do, where they lead, where or what they plant? And isn't fear the opposite? And by extension, isn't to be fearful to be faithless?

The Scriptures shape the meaning of *faith*: to have faith in God is to so fully trust in him that we don't assume we have other options. We put all our eggs into one basket. Christians put their lives, their totality, into trusting that what he promises and who he claims to be is true. What if it isn't? What if he isn't? Then we've got nowhere to turn. If God doesn't show up, we're sunk.

If I'm certain, I don't need to exercise faith. Frankly, much of what we do could be done by someone who doesn't believe in God.

The term *faith*, worn thin by careless usage and trite claims, loses its wonder and power. Look again at Joshua. When he bumped up against the Jordan, pushed by tired Israelites who wanted access to the Promised Land, he asked of the Lord, "What am I to do?" "When the feet of the priests touch the water, I'll stop it," was the reply. Joshua might have said,

"Interesting. But I have another idea. You stop the water and then we'll walk across."

Faith is what we do. It's being vulnerable enough to trust. It means we proceed without a plan B. Too often we assume we're living by faith, but just in case, we'll build a bridge or two. Certainty is good. Faith is different. It's the opposite: to have faith is to operate in a zone that casts us beyond our capabilities and capacities.

Faith is the exercise of the will to do that which requires God's help to succeed.

IMPORTANCE OF FAITH

To you, as leader, faith matters. It is a powerful force in leading. It is an indispensable tool that brings plans, organization, resources, and community to life. It is true partnership, and when those you lead see you humbly trusting the provision of the Lord, it heightens their awareness that they too need to walk by faith. Here is what faith does.

FAITH CHARACTERIZES LEADERSHIP

In my experience people gifted to lead usually exercise faith. This is not to say that good leaders must by nature be risk takers. But the exercise of faith does help identify people who, by their gifts, are willing to move beyond the status quo and explore new and difficult fields. In recruiting personnel for positions in which leadership, as distinguished from management, is needed, I look for candidates who have the emotional capacity to move outside of the habitual and explore new avenues without the need for predictability.

FAITH BRINGS GOD INTO PLAY

Risk-taking is not only for people of Christian faith. However, it is important to note that for a Christian the role of belief—in that I trust in the provision and presence of God—is critical. Faith is taking action on that belief, and that brings God into play in what I do. Would the water have parted if the priests had not entered the Jordan? As much as they believed God would or could have stopped the river flow, without their action of faith it is safe to assume the water would not have parted.

I return to my earlier question: why is it that *without faith it is impossible to please God*?

Interactivity with God is at the core of human life. Our imprint is *imago Dei*: made in his image. God interacts. That is core to the Hebrew/Christian understanding of his nature. In physical creation, humans are made to interface with God. We are constructed for fellowship and interactivity. Though we may have an entrepreneurial streak, the Genesis record notes that "in the cool of the day" human–God interface was normal fare. We were made to be together.

Added to that relationship is a responsibility for humans to work, to do, to manage, to oversee. Not as separate or within another sphere but in partnership. Notwithstanding the cleavage brought by human moral failure, that mandate has not been set aside.

Here is where faith makes a difference. If what we set out to do can be done without help from God, in that sense we don't need him. Operating within our own skills and drive, we take risks, needing hope to succeed.

The difference with Christian enterprise—and I include all enterprises that Christians lead, not only "religious" organizations—is that we include in our sphere of life the reality of God interfacing with us. This is more than a nod of the head to God. It is a dynamic. We please God by moving in faith, knowing that without his enablement we'll fail. In that sense we bring God into play. We please God as our faith brings us together in ways beyond simply a belief. It is one thing to say, "Yes, I believe you will help me"; it is something else to say, "I won't make it without your help."

There is a thrill in going beyond what most see as doable, energized by the uncertainty of the initiative, calling for determined and creative efforts. Taking risks and experiencing faith are naturally linked. But there is a downside.

I discovered at times that what I described as faith was what another, who operates outside of trusting in God, would call risk. I'd construct a plan so that if God didn't show up, I'd still succeed. I conditioned the activity to ensure that the goal was reached. I figured out how it could be done without God's assistance.

That is not faith. Faith is risking but with an understanding that partnership with God is essential. I don't go it alone. I set out from my securities of both past and present with the compass of faith, operating on the assumption that God is essential to the plan. Faith isn't what I feel or believe. It is what I will and do.

FAITH TRANSFORMS US

We look to leaders to inspire us with their great ideas. We may grumble about aspects of personality but we need their vision and energy to help us see the bigger picture and to remind us of where we are going and what really matters.

What about the leaders? Where do they get inspiration to create the grander design, and where do they derive energy to fuel those they lead?

◆ ◆ ◆

My first full-time ministry employment landed us in Montreal, called to a ministry serving young people and those in trouble with the law. It was following the Expo '67 World's Fair extravaganza, the like of which Canada had never known.

It coincided with a political debate raging in Canada. The province of Quebec, fueled by a separatist uprising, was about to fall prey to a movement that not only killed a politician and kidnapped a foreign diplomat but set a course to separate from Canada.

This debate between "the two solitudes" had been brewing for years; however, the excitement of Expo '67 deflected attention from it. As the world's fair came to an end and the political debate intensified, English-speaking Canadians left the province of Quebec in droves.

We moved into Montreal that summer as vans were moving families out. The youth ministry had unwisely invested in an assortment of programs during Expo and ended up, in effect, insolvent, a new word for me as a theology and history major.

Along with that were two issues I had no experience in handling: the youth culture was about to undergo a massive overhaul (called the counterculture), and the financial and volunteer base of the youth ministry was being lost to the provincial political debate as many people left.

As leader, even though young, overwhelmed, and unsure of what to do, I was looked to by older and wiser people who, having asked me to come, now expected me to lead.

I could not have had a better orientation to learning leadership. I relied on four things: instinct, what I had learned from my father, a deep conviction that the Lord had led us to Montreal, and people who encouraged and helped me.

On the edge of disaster, uncertain of how to proceed, we experimented. Some ideas worked; others failed. But in the doing I learned that faith is like a muscle: you use it or lose it. Little by little the debt was reduced. Fear of further failure was overcome as volunteers witnessed small moments of success. I had no map with roads or distances. Instead I was handed a compass.

I learned the elemental factors of faith, and it started me out on a lifelong learning track of keeping faith central as I led.

◆ ◆ ◆

Faith is not a single act. It is the Spirit's work in personal transformation. Though an essential "muscle," faith isn't given to us to make us better leaders. By it, God brings us into a closer and more participatory relationship so we will enter into the life and work of the trinity.

Exercising faith moves me to a new level of knowing God. Faith connects us to the heart of God in unique and important ways.

FAITH TRANSFORMS OTHERS

The exercise of faith extends into transforming others. It isn't a solo performance. It is not for myself; nor is it for a limited benefit. As much as Abraham and Sarah may have wanted a child for their own fulfillment, ultimately the birth of Isaac was the beginning of a race to be a light to the world. Faith sees beyond self. It views the activity of God in what we are doing as a means of spreading out life to those we lead.

FAITH PROVIDES A MODEL FOR VISION CASTING.

Knowing that our lives operate within the space of God's care gives permission for leadership to press the boundaries, even of credulity. In short, because our visions are not just our own ideas limited by our capacity, they embody greater possibilities.

FAITH MOVES US FROM SECURITY INTO NEW TERRITORY

Inertia, which keeps us from exploring beyond where we are, is a kind of "unfaith," a predisposition to remain in our securities. Some personalities are more amenable to moving outside protecting fences. While the Spirit uses these restless personalities, faith moves up to a different level than that: faith is moving out based on a trust in God's help.

Stories of biblical characters operating in faith often describe them as leaving, moving, going out from family and tribal identity. It's as if the actual picking up of belongings and family opened them to a new level of trust beyond what they would have known if they had remained with familiar people and places.

Abraham left the leading-edge culture of his day. Leaving his home was more than saying goodbye to family; it was putting behind him a world of scientific advances—including the invention of cuneiform, a means of keeping records permanent.

When I picked up the few files of the EFC and started on a journey that eventually led to publishing a magazine, launching a national voice on vital issues, hosting a weekly national television program, and opening a national office in Ottawa, I began with a simple decision to invest my future and the security of our family in an idea outside of my life experience. I had learned how to create and manage youth ministry, but this was different. I didn't know what to do. So I began by publishing a national magazine. I had just had my first book published, which had given me at least a journalism 101 course but not much beyond that. I had to learn. And as I reached out for help, there were new opportunities to explore.

Faith opens doors to new realities. Imagine opening a door to a hallway. You are faced with a choice: to return or continue. You choose to move along the hallway, testing the occasional door. To your surprise some open to opportunities you would have missed if you had stopped at the first door. They came to sight only when you made the first move. Faith is like that. It is an inclination to try new doors.

It isn't that there are too few worlds to conquer; it's that too many people stay locked into their current world, unwilling to open that first door.

FAITH PREPARES LEADERS FOR THE NEXT STAGE

Doing is essential in learning. Most actions of faith go unnoticed by others. We learn by a frequent flexing of faith. As we exercise, moving forward in faith becomes less frightening than when we infrequently or never tested faith. Martin Luther King gave his great Washington speech after years of testing his faith in marches, prisons, and in the face of those determined to destroy his vision. Abraham came to the place of accepting the unbelievable call to sacrifice his son after decades of walking in concert with this God he had come to trust. One stage leads to the next, but without risk-taking today you won't be ready for the next.

FAITH FACILITATES INTERACTION WITH GOD

Earlier I noted that faith, as an activity, brings God into play in one's life. Here let's take it a step further. Faith not only is interaction, it perpetuates interaction: the exercise of faith stimulates the desire to continue in faith. Leading without faith becomes drab, boring, and lifeless. Leaders can easily drift, losing the interface with the God we can't see. It isn't long, then, before we are off doing our own thing, in our way, in our strength, in our time. Faith draws us back. Putting ourselves into places where faith is the only means of moving forward brings us back into interactivity that transforms and renews.

FAITH CREATES NEW REALITIES

Faith makes something out of what wasn't there. It creates. Bringing together people, resources, and ideas, faith synergistically combines ingredients to bring about something new or renewed.

God's creation isn't a world ruled by a zero-sum equation. There is no limit on ideas. Resources given to one doesn't mean there are fewer resources for another. Brain specialists remind us we use only a portion of our capacity; so too is it with exercising faith—there are no limits for us in leading important and valuable initiatives.

HOW FAITH WORKS

Clarity on the meaning of faith helps to set faith apart from other aspects of the journey. To help further identify the nature and importance of faith in leading, let's view the actions of Nehemiah.

FAITH IS AN ACTION

Faith is an action. It is what we do. Because of how we befuddle the word, its elementary meaning gets lost in belief, feelings, hope, and the many emotions that fill our religious life.

Nehemiah learned about the state of his homeland, the frightful vulnerability of the Temple, and the embarrassment this brought to his people. His story pivots around his request to the king for time and assistance in the rebuilding. It was a major risk-taking moment. The king might have suspected treachery. Nehemiah, as cupbearer, was counted on as the final person the king trusted. Crafty and always observant, the king lived by his ability to observe and discern. So when he saw something bothering this trusted servant, it would not have been far down his list to ask himself if Nehemiah was up to no good. In that moment Nehemiah acted in faith. He risked everything by trusting that the God he had spent time with was with him as he acted.

FAITH WORKS ON INNER CONVICTION

The activity of faith often includes our emotions. Given that how we feel influences our decision-making, the exercising of faith is linked with emotions as we make choices based on convictions of belief and vision.

Nehemiah had such passion about the well-being of his home and people, and their strategic importance within the economy of God that when notified of their struggles, he knew what he was to do. Faith was a natural extension of that inner life.

FAITH RESTS ON A HISTORY OF TRUSTING GOD

Faith doesn't come out of nowhere. It is built on a history of trusting God. Nehemiah wasn't a novice when he made the daring move before the king. His life had been tutored in a theology and experience with people that gave him a repository of understanding.

As my grandson Zachary—son of our daughter, Muriel, and her husband, Jesse—and I were playing, the two-year-old couldn't get enough of our rough-and-tumble fun. The higher I threw him in the air, the more he loved it. If we did it once, he wanted it a hundred times. However, the first time, he screamed with fright. Then he realized Papa had caught him. There was no danger. He now could put his life in my hands. He had a history of trust. And that trust leads to other activities of trust.

FAITH LEARNS FROM OTHERS

Leaders learn from others, and there is no better way than to observe how faith is at work in others and then to see how it can be replicated in us. Nehemiah had a long list of patriarchs from whom he drew stories of faith. From stories often retold by his people, he recited their acts of faith. He saw the effects on the Jewish tribes, both when leaders failed and when they were heroic. He had patterns that stood him in good stead in the moment when it was his turn to exercise faith.

FAITH IS ROOTED IN BIBLICAL KNOWLEDGE

Faith rises out of a heart sufficiently rooted in biblical text. Faith as a constituent in the wide range of human activities is not limited to people of biblical faith. It is an activity that moves people into risk-taking that is exercised by people of all faiths and of no faith. A skydiver has faith in the ability of the parachute to land him safely. The skydiver's faith in God has nothing to do with that faith (apart from faith in the laws of physics). Likewise a businessperson investing in a product takes a risk, exercising faith in the product or the people producing it.

There is a different dimension to faith rooted in belief in a God who is both creator and sustainer. This elevates activity to a different level. While one may rightly trust in a product, a system, or another person, the act of putting one's faith in God for interactivity is unique.

We know this God in whom we trust from our reading of Scripture. Embedded in the texts are stories that become the basis for belief. I earlier noted that belief is cognitive and definable. Faith is not that, yet it is founded on belief, the platform from which faith makes its move.

EXERCISING FAITH

Where does one begin to exercise faith?

START SMALL

As with any exercise, start carefully, and over time you will grow in endurance and strength. Our first ministry assignment landed me in financial duress, which forced me to think about faith as an element of leadership. The learning was huge. But it taught me how to exercise faith within a plan and strategy.

ALIGN WITH THE SPIRIT

If you are serious about moving out of the boundaries of your current world, pray what Bob Pierce, founder of World Vision, prayed: Lord, break my heart with the things that break your heart.

Such a prayer will make you vulnerable to God's concerns, putting yourself in line with the Spirit's agenda. Beware, such a prayer may lead you to places of risk and challenge.

EXERCISE

I'm not trivializing faith as if it were *only* a muscle of the will. Faith, in its origin and object, is found in God. We don't will ourselves. It is an activity of the Spirit through which we effect, by our choice, his enablement. Recall the progression of faith-building moments during the life of Moses. His first recorded act, killing an Egyptian, sent him scurrying into the hills. It was only after forty years of walking in a different world that he was trusted to approach Pharaoh. But that too was progressive. Despite his fear of personal incompetence, step by step he developed an understanding and accompanying ability to exercise faith on behalf of his people.

PLAN

Faith is not isolated. It is a part of an overall plan. Developing a business plan is integral to exercising faith. By "plan" I don't mean a backup system in case the step of faith doesn't work. Planning ensures that the exercise of faith fits within a wider vision and allows the accomplishments of faith to be supported and in turn contribute to an ongoing viable and worthwhile activity.

PRACTICE HUMILITY

The inherent danger of God meeting us at the river of faith is that when it becomes public that the exercise of faith produced a visible result, egos can become inflated. Praise is heaped on the person exercising faith rather than on the source and object of faith.

So what does one do? Practice being humble. The biblical call is "Humble yourself" (James 4:10). Whether you feel humble is not the point. Our emotions ebb and flow, and often we have no understanding why. Humility, like faith, is what we exercise by the will. Is Billy Graham humble? I can't say whether he felt humble, but I do know that he acted with humility. And what we do filters back into what we are.

DISCERNING FAITH

How do I discern whether the faith I am exercising is authentic or merely personal wishes? There are a few rules to use in discernment.

FAITH BECOMES A WAY OF LIFE

First, exercising faith is not a single, once-in-a-lifetime event. It is a way of life. The incremental activity of faith makes it part of one's normal walk. It doesn't become an all-or-nothing moment. There may be times when the exercise of faith is larger than usual, but faith is a gift we get used to exercising.

FAITH ALIGNS WITH SCRIPTURE

Test the purpose of your act of faith with Scripture. See if it lines up with the Bible's ethical and moral criteria. If you are exercising faith for building a larger church to show others the rightness of your theology, that will make your "faith" suspect. If you are exercising faith so your company will grow larger so that you will need less to trust the Lord, I'd say that too is suspect.

FAITH BEARS SCRUTINY

Test the situation of your faith with others. You may be reluctant to tell others about it, fearful they may poke holes in it. Faith with God's imprimatur deserves the light of day. If the plan is plausible as an exercise of faith, it can stand scrutiny. By so subjecting it to examination, you will build a stronger rationale.

FAITH FITS INTO THE WIDER SCENE

Don't ignore Athens: identify a logical sequence. Though the scientific logic and human rationality of Athens can impede the faith-driven life of Jerusalem, logic and rationality are two indispensable gifts of creation. Identify where the faith-driven portion fits within the wider scene. Make sure it won't become simply an appendage to the plan. As I nurtured my wife's word on the new property for Tyndale, we exercised faith as we saw it as part of a larger educational plan to train people for service in the world.

FAITH HAS ULTIMATE VALUE

Answer this question: What do I expect will be the outcomes and value of this exercise of faith? Project out to the end, and visualize what it might accomplish and its value. For Nehemiah, the expected outcome was clear: finish the wall to protect the Temple. However, within the struggle of opposition, grumpy workers, and the heat and dust of the day, he would have to remind himself and others that what they were doing was a good thing. It would have value in the end.

Defining the end value before you begin helps to verify and validate the exercise.

Getting there requires learning the nature of faith, an important part of the leadership process. Nehemiah understood that without God's interaction in his plan, the idea had no chance of success.

PRINCIPLE 4

Discover the Value Proposition

You may be rebuilding a broken-down wall or constructing a new wall. In either case defining your value proposition—the core around which your enterprise operates—is vital in design and construction.

Nehemiah's value proposition was to preserve the witness of God's people. While the immediate need was to solve Jerusalem's security problem by rebuilding the walls, the core value was the life of faith. Walls were needed to protect the value proposition.

◆ ◆ ◆

In 1983 I was invited to lead the Evangelical Fellowship of Canada, a national Christian association of Protestant churches, denominations, and mission agencies. Formed in the mid 1960s, it had yet to develop into a viable organization.

Early in my tenure, Terry Law, founder of World Compassion and personal friend, challenged me: "In fifteen words or less, what is your mission?"

I stumbled and fumbled. I didn't know. There were many things I thought this national association could do. But I hadn't landed on its value proposition. What was our reason for being? This is critical for any organization, but more so in this case because much of the popular perception of evangelicals in Canada was formed by images and caricatures beamed to us from south of the border.

Canadians are both blessed and plagued by many U.S. voices. Many a home is permanently tuned to U.S. news broadcasts. Some Canadians seem to exhibit a greater familiarity with U.S. government than with Canadian.

Though today there is a better understanding of matters of religion and faith, too often Canadian media simply replace "American" with "Canadian" and funnel to the Canadian audience perceptions originating in the U.S., perpetuating the impression that the views U.S. Christians hold are synonymous with those of Canadians.

In 1980 Ronald Reagan, leading the conservative movement, had been elected as U.S. president. In the run-up to the next election, televangelist Jerry Falwell and his Moral Majority were particularly effective in getting media attention, influencing voters and warning Americans of encroaching liberalism. The term "fundamentalism" rankled evangelicals in Canada. It was pejorative, raising specters of extremism.

Canadians were divided over this religious ruckus south of the border, especially as Falwell was becoming the de facto spokesperson for evangelicals throughout North America. Some Canadians resonated with his ideas; others were offended. Regardless of varying opinions, Canadian evangelicals had no one to thank but ourselves. We had not developed voices to speak for us. It was evident something had to be done in Canada, or by default the U.S. voice would become ours.

A couple of years earlier, the EFC executive had asked me, as a volunteer, to survey Canadian evangelicals on their expectations of the EFC. Overwhelmingly, responses identified the need for a Canadian voice.

I traveled across the country hearing about issues that leaders identified as needing attention. Foundational to them all was a view that had long outlived its reality: an assumption that a Christian consensus existed between Christians and Canadian public leaders. Whatever had been was now gone. Leaders in the public square showed little interest in shaping Canada from a Christian understanding of life. Unfortunately evangelicals assumed we could get on with our life and ministry (evangelism, building churches, engaging in world missions) and trust public leaders, our cultural gatekeepers, to run the country based on Christian assumptions and values.

How wrong we were. In the past that approach had fit well with our view of mission—to focus on preparing people for eternity. It had also fit with our view that matters outside our definition of church mission—such as managing our nation—were not our concern. We were satisfied to leave it to those from older, mainline churches to oversee our country along the lines of what we assumed was a continuing consensus of general Christian values. Such thinking was deadly.

We discovered our value proposition as we asked, How can we shift Canadian evangelical thinking to a wider awareness of God's agenda, including engagement in public life?

The legal and social context of Canada was undergoing a profound change. The Supreme Court struck down Section 251 of the Criminal Code, relating to abortion. Abortionist Dr. Henry Morgentaler took the issue to the court and won—the first major test of the criminal code under the Charter of Rights and Freedoms, passed in 1982. As much as the charter had been debated, it was just a set of ideas until those ideas were tested by courts and established in law as legal precedents. Only then would we really know what the ideas meant and how they might intersect with Canadian life.

The Morgentaler decision galvanized the evangelical community. Though the effect of the charter with respect to the Morgentaler decision might not have been what Parliament had in mind, the decision left a clear impression in the minds of evangelical leaders that life would not go on as before.

Terry's question was a triggering moment. After a few false starts, we identified our value proposition, which gave clarity to the role of the EFC and offered a sense of mission and strategy to our supporting public. We reduced the value proposition to this declaration of purpose: to be a voice for evangelicals. For the next decade and a half, that became the organization's mantra, including these essential ingredients: to be articulate, to be thoughtful, to be Christlike, to be educated, to be responsible.

Ambiguity was gone. Everything we did was measured against this value proposition. In time we worked out a more broadly defined mission and vision, but still under the aegis of "being a voice." As people understood, it brought increased support.

◆ ◆ ◆

How do you go about learning your value proposition?

LOCATE THE ESSENCE

Try these steps:

1. Brainstorm with three groups:

   a. Insiders—senior members of the organization, including regular donors

   b. Peripherals—those with a more casual acquaintance, including occasional donors

   c. Outsiders—those who may know about you but have no organizational or financial involvement

2. In separate meetings, ask questions:

   a. What is the essence of our history?

   b. What do we do best?

   c. What do we not do well?

   d. What should we do that we aren't now doing?

   e. Who else is doing what we are doing?

   f. Are they doing it better, and if so, why?

3. Allow time to reflect on the responses, cataloging them for reference.

4. The exact wording is important. Take time to get it right, doing edit after edit until it fits with mission and rings with clarity.

TRUST THE SPIRIT

Management can too easily be carried out without regard to the life of the Spirit, for there is more going on than what we know, estimate, or expect.

As God guides us in moments of darkness and times of the unknown, the Spirit undertakes to support and fulfill the agenda we have agreed on in faith.

He knows your vision and passion and where it will lead.

DIG BENEATH THE CLUTTER OF
SHORT-TERM GOALS

In the course of three rebuilding experiences, and in locating value, mission, and calling, I've noted that many organizations operate on short-term goals. Then as problems increase, survival—defined by immediate goals—becomes the reoccurring theme. To keep from being stuck in a survival mode, begin with the question "How did we begin?"

When we bring in resources, we understandably take the "lowest-hanging fruit" first, forgetting that it takes more effort to reach resources at the next level. Further, when the higher fruit is gone, nothing is left until the next harvest. Also, fruit trees don't bear forever, and if we have not planted new trees to start maturing before the old ones die out, we'll end up with no fruit at all. Scrambling to meet this year's budget may obscure what budgets are about, which is to help us make it this year and the next, and the next.

One organization was overjoyed to receive a large bequest, just enough to cover the current year's deficit, viewing it rightly as a provision of the Lord. However, they got trapped in thinking of the immediate, forgetting you can't set budgets based on the assumption that further bequests will pick up future shortfalls. So ask, Is the financial plan sustainable in the coming years?

To stick with the orchard metaphor, a fruit farmer sometimes encounters circumstances beyond human control, such as climate change or shifts in market demand. These may require significant adaptation in how things are done or even what fruit is grown to meet demand.

When situations arise for which no solutions have been identified and implemented, people adjust and survive for a year or so and even maintain a livable equilibrium, but in time they will succumb. Leaders are responsible not only for finding ways to multiply resources to provide for lean years but also for diversifying so an expanding base will allow growth.

What keeps organizations from thinking for the long term? It is easy to fall prey to the passion of your vision, refusing to countenance possible threats. Trouble and crosswinds are inevitable, even in the best of ministries. Leadership can't anticipate all possible unfavorable factors, but by designing into the organization rigorous reflection and examination, you build capacity to anticipate and recognize approaching trouble.

BE ON THE LOOKOUT FOR RESISTANCE

Nehemiah faced resistance from deniers, malcontents, fierce opponents, and gainsayers. Leaders tell stories of resisters: opposing what was done, how it was done, and its rationale.

As you poke about the fallen walls, the resistance you encounter may provide clues as to the importance of what you are doing. For Nehemiah, the outside resistance made it clear that protecting the Temple and the City of David posed a threat to the surrounding peoples, which made it clear why it needed protection. Opposition pointed the way.

Peter Koestenbaum, in *Overcoming Resistance,* draws a parallel between leading and driving. Both actions must overcome resistance to move forward. In moving an organization toward health, you will inevitably face resistance that could disable, undo, and block. He notes three dynamics that contribute to resistance in mission: the psychodynamic, systemic, and existential forms.

PSYCHODYNAMIC RESISTANCE

Life experiences inflict emotional hangovers and debilitating memories that may lead a person in the organization to oppose a given action or proposal. Childhood and young-adult experiences can generate conflict.

A number of us involved in Christian ministry (men only on this occasion) met for a three-day prayer summit, spending our time in reflective prayer, Bible reading, hymn singing, and interactive prayer.

Occasionally we placed a chair in the center and invited anyone to occupy it, confess a need, request a prayer, or be silent. One senior leader took the chair and told of a heartbreaking and dysfunctional relationship with his father. We listened, then gathered around in prayer. Soon another took the chair and told a similar story. Then another, who had never heard his father say how proud he was of his son. This went on all afternoon, with most of the thirty-five men openly describing lingering sorrow in life because of poor relationships with fathers.

Throughout life we accumulate experiences that shape us. Leaders aren't called on to be the in-house therapists, but as we meet unfair and irresponsible resistance, we need to remember that there may be reasons for people's behavior that have little to do with the immediate situation.

SYSTEMIC RESISTANCE

Systems get stuck. People do too, believing their actions are best. People who are inwardly focused may be unaware that others also have valued opinions.

An organization can get into trouble when it is unduly constrained by groups who measure life by political correctness or the status quo, willing to pull most any lever to stop new thinking from having a say.

We experienced systemic resistance in restructuring a nineteenth-century Bible college into a twenty-first-century Christian university. The change came about through a reassessment of the value proposition. The Bible college movement that began in the 1890s served churches, missions, and service agencies very well. Toward the end of the twentieth century that changed as seminaries became the prime place for training leaders for church and mission ministry. Many young people who attended Bible colleges did so for personal spiritual enrichment. That also changed as young people wanted degrees that would transfer into other university-based programs. However, those who chose Bible college intending to go into a ministry vocation but then later changed their minds, ended up with degrees that had little marketplace currency. The building of Christian universities solved those problems: they provided spiritual nurturing and biblical training along with degrees that allowed graduates to move into professions. In short, they were approved and accepted by the public marketplace of education and work. But there was pushback. People feared a liberalization of content and purpose.

Anticipating questions on why we would change, we drew lessons from other schools that had migrated to a Christian university focus, and we decided that the best way to resolve those concerns was to get out in front of the question and answer it with our value proposition. We told our community what we were doing, why it was important, and where it would lead. We did this at every opportunity—events, donor letters, banquets, graduation, church services, and pastoral and parent meetings.

EXISTENTIAL RESISTANCE

Some people who are resistant to a different worldview fear that another idea may be of more value than theirs. Anxiety sets in. Fueled by insecurity, their feelings can pressure an organization to become protective and isolationistic, out of touch and unaware.

Tinkering with an organization's purpose and structure may not be sufficient. Bringing in a new idea may not, of itself, bring a turnaround. At the
heart is the need to change. The biblical term is *metanoia*, literally meaning new birth, or birth from above.

◆ ◆ ◆

*The rebirth of YFC taught me much about overcoming existential resis-
tance.*

*Youth for Christ had risen dramatically in the post World War II period.
Young people, matured early by the war experience, returned home to a
moribund church. YFC, started in the U.S. by Billy Graham and in Canada
by Charles Templeton, was dramatic and life altering. It brought about
change. However, in a couple of decades, it too got stuck.*

*YFC events in Saskatoon were central to my younger years. Nothing
matched the twice-a-month Saturday-night rally. However, when Lily and
I moved to Montreal in 1967, the counterrevolution of the hippy days was
underway. Young people listened to music other than that of George
Beverly Shea and the Blackwood Brothers Quartet. A generation had
passed, and young people had little understanding of the gospel, its stories,
metaphors, and theology.*

*Faced with a new generation, we knew the old format wasn't working, yet
our mission to reach young people had not changed. So what to do? Those
who had led YFC in its first generation seemed obstinate, clearly disap-
proving of our new approaches. New music was labeled "worldly."*

*Not only was there a shift in the popular youth culture, an increasing num-
ber of young people were in trouble with the law, which called for a kind of
ministry that didn't have the flair or stage presence of the old-time rallies.*

*It was in that context that we rebirthed the ministry. It was tough. Some
leaders left. Many donors, thinking we were compromising the gospel,
mailed their support elsewhere. Yet over time, fundamental change came
into play. While many supporters from the previous era were unwilling to
accept the new focus or formats, a new generation of leaders, board members, and supporters embraced the change. Metanoia was in play.*

*The value proposition was framed by this motto: Geared to the times;
anchored to the Rock. It sustained us in recreating ministry, generation*

after generation. It was painful, long term, and upsetting, yet we learned to identify and hold on to our value proposition. More than a half century later, YFC continues to adapt, anticipating change, creatively developing ministries that deal with real issues, all the while remaining solidly linked to its continuing value proposition.

◆ ◆ ◆

INSTALL THE RIGHT KIND OF LEADERSHIP

Even when you figure out your value proposition, without the right kind of leadership you won't get far. A crisis doesn't call for an "on-the-one-hand-and-on-the-other-hand" kind of leader. It needs one who takes hold and moves with energy and determination.

In the crisis at Tyndale, we had sixty days before fall semester was to begin. Faculty and staff wondered whether they should look elsewhere for employment, and students were checking out what schools would accept transfer credits. I couldn't say, "Give me a few days and I'll get back to you." It was now or not at all.

Leaders make decisions. Theories of applied leadership, creative and helpful as they are, give way to determined and often intuitive initiatives in crunch times. In reading books on leadership, I invariably check the flyleaf to see if the author has ever led.

There are two sides to this leadership equation: developing a well-thought-out strategy and learning to operate intuitively. Every leader inclines to one side or the other. Bob Pierce, the charismatic, passionate, and intuitive founder of World Vision, began that international organization with a promise to fund an orphan's monthly needs until adulthood. Pierce's powerful storytelling invited others to do the same. The organization grew beyond anyone's expectations. But it was also limited by his impulsive shifts of plans and priorities. Eventually he was released. Tragic as it seemed at the time, that the founder and president would be turned out of the organization he had birthed, only by his release did it grow into the worldwide institution it is now, giving him freedom to establish The Samaritan's Purse, a quick response-agency to help those in disaster.

It took someone else, Ted Engstrom, much the opposite type of leader, to craft it into what it has become. Having had his leadership and organizational learning honed in Youth for Christ, Engstrom was schooled in planning and strategizing. His tenure proved the critical turning point in World Vision's history.

It often takes a bull-in-the-china-shop personality to birth an idea, but only for a time.

BUILD ON THE ESSENCE

Finding the essence—the value proposition—of the organization is the beginning. Now begins leading the organization into what it might be.

NURTURE SPIRITUAL LIFE

As leader, you are the one to articulate spiritual understanding and expectations. If your skills are not in speaking, you may be inclined to delegate that to someone else. But don't delegate the responsibility of keeping spiritual matters in view. Leadership necessitates that you oversee the reading of the spiritual temperature of your people and keep the flame lit.

Christian organizations are particularly vulnerable to spiritual drift, losing focus or even memory of their value proposition. This can occur at two levels. The first is the organizational mission and ethos. James Tunstead Burtchaell's book *The Dying of the Light: The Disengagement of Colleges and Universities from their Christian Churches* describes how major U.S. universities, born in a time of spiritual reformation, slid down the slope of expediency. As they grew and became more established, leadership, faculty, and students became increasingly uncomfortable with the faith that had inspired their beginnings. So rather than clarify and retain their original spiritual commitment, they compromised, allowing the institutions to find ways of accommodating student expectations with no linkage to spiritual commitment.

Humanitarian organizations face the danger of accommodating religious and political pressures while downplaying their spiritual roots. David Toycen, president of World Vision Canada, told me, "The leader is responsible to ensure the expression of Christian faith and to nurture staff." Part of his plan is daily chapel and a weekly senior staff meeting for prayer, where they pray through lists of needs and share personal issues in the organization. It gives senior staff the opportunity to help each other on their spiritual journeys. In addition, a full day is set apart as a day of prayer once a year.

The second level is the day-to-day routine. A Christian agency that doesn't have space in its schedule for devotional time will soon lose its spiritual base. As much as documents may proclaim an organization's spiritual heritage, without actual prayer, Bible reading, and devotionals, its spirituality will be on paper only.

How does a leader protect against spiritual drift? There are factors a leader can take into consideration in shoring up the spiritual life of the community.

RIGHT HIRES

The proper screening of those we bring into leadership is the most important means of being foundational in faith. At Tyndale we knew that, as a Christian university and seminary, we would win or lose based on whom we hired to teach.

Within the sphere of recruitment and employment, you will run up against all sorts of resistance, everywhere from courts to recruitment agencies. Documents will try to ensure people's compliance with the organization's theology, attendance at chapel, the importance of Christian character and behavior, but they provide no guarantee. Our mission statement was clear. Our statement of faith was unequivocal. Yet we know that people can slip into an organization, saying they believe one thing yet being lackadaisical in faith.

When hiring, have applicants write out their understanding of the mission statement. Make it fundamental to the process of recruitment. Not only will this imprint on their minds its importance, it will bring those who are recruiting and evaluating face to face with what the organization claims to be—and who they are in relation to it.

RENEWAL OF MISSION COMMITMENT

Don't assume everyone catches or retains the central, driving mission. It needs yearly reinforcing, specific efforts to remind personnel what you are about. Make the mission statement part of the annual staff review. Ask for a one-page reflection on how a person's work during the past year assisted in meeting the organization's mission. In a staff retreat, break up into smaller groups and ask each group to first identify ways the group is fulfilling the mission and then offer suggestions on how implementing it might be improved.

Renewal of Spiritual Core

Resisting spiritual drift requires strategic activity. Regular activity is critical. Returning to the World Vision experience, this agency wrestles with issues of pluralism, human rights, and finding able staff from various religious communities. Even so, it continues to hold chapel, unapologetic in its Christian heart, theology, and passion.

Don't assume that because you are known as a Christian organization or church and operate with a Christian mission, the heart of Christ will continue to reside habitually in the operation. It takes careful nurturing and oversight.

CULTIVATION OF VISION

What happens when you've lost the vision, when leading is drudgery, when the days begin with a gnawing fear that either you've been trapped into something that won't work or you've been asked to do what you aren't geared to do: in effect, you know the value proposition but it no longer fuels you?

◆ ◆ ◆

Twice in my ministry career I lost vision. The first was while serving as president of Youth for Christ. I got bored. I didn't know it at the time. But it got me into trouble.

The Canadian youth agency was built on local chapters defined by boundaries of municipalities. Each chapter was responsible to develop a board of directors, implement ministry, maintain standards, and recruit support. The national office supplied the chapters with training, counsel, and management and facilitated new ministry ideas. As well, it was responsible for developing new chapters and expanding the ministry across the country.

As president, my motivation was to expand YFC across Canada. Senior staff jokingly said, "Don't let Stiller out of the office or he'll open another chapter we will have to manage."

Unwittingly I moved into new territory that I thought was in keeping with the role of the national office. I wrote my first book, A Generation Under Siege, *thinking it fitting for a national youth leader. The problem was that staff didn't understand how that fit into our strategy and my calling. They interpreted it as me being distracted. Then I worked with other agencies to develop a national youth congress. Senior staff saw this as further evidence that I was losing interest in our core calling. Only in leaving did I understand what was going on. After sixteen years I needed new horizons. Sometimes it is better to leave, better for the organization and for you.*

The second time, I saw it coming. I felt the weariness of my work. Weekends were a relief, for then I could preach. This came some years into my presidency at Tyndale. I didn't know how long I could continue.

Our team had rescued the college and seminary in the mid 1990s. We got it out of debt. We changed the name. We redeveloped the college into a university. The Lord opened the door for us to purchase an outstanding campus in Toronto. The Spirit had brought me into circumstances that I could hardly leave. As well, I was constrained by the earlier call, by a commitment to our board chair, and by realization that it wasn't the right time to leave.

There are times when we simply muscle forward. Boredom, fatigue, or morning dread is not, in and of itself, a signal one should leave. If I had left at that point, it would have interrupted the Spirit's work to bring together a plan, people, and resources.

There were factors that enabled me to find passion in the value proposition.

I kept close connection with a trusted friend, Norm Allen, and a small group of peers who provided me with the emotional support and personal friendship I needed, regularly and on call. Norm grouped seven of us, all in similar leadership roles, and we met twice a year on retreat. Around the table and in times of spiritual reflection we opened our hearts to others who could listen and help.

Then I ensured that I had outlets for preaching. When learning that I preached three weekends a month, someone asked, "Do you need the offerings?" "No," I replied, "an audience." Preaching allowed me to develop sermons; it provided ministry so I could speak into lives and participate in a time of inspiration. Some weeks I lived for these opportunities.

Also I worked at supporting senior leadership. Delegation has been one of my strong suits—in fact, at times too much, for staff sometimes thought I was uninterested in their work. A logical and well-cared-for schedule can make all the difference. Organizing my schedule allowed me to ensure that key meetings with the leadership team, individually and as a group, were carefully mapped out and managed.

FIND A BROKEN WALL

The task of raising capital provided me with demands that helped generate passion. To be able to raise more money for a project than had ever been done in Canadian church history pressed me to a creative edge.

◆ ◆ ◆

I have no reliable formula for how leaders might deal with boredom, fatigue, or burnout. But I have learned that the following may help.

- ◆ Find one or a small group of highly trusted friends.

- ◆ Find one part of your gifting that renews and refreshes you, and make sure that is a part of your schedule.

- ◆ Work your schedule. Don't fall into it. Think about what is needed, when and how often. If possible, have someone manage it for you, making appointments and inevitable changes. Keep your distance from the process. Decide who you need to see, when, and for what reason, and let someone else set it up.

- ◆ If your tendency is managerial, put into your schedule something creative that forces you to meet new demands, stretching you beyond the usual.

- ◆ There are, however, situations when leaving the ministry is best for all. And leaving earlier rather than later is generally better.

UTILIZE EVERY CRISIS

When crisis comes, as it inevitably will, see it as an opportunity. Tragedy is often the turning point for success. Amid the rubble of failed dreams arise ideas that otherwise might never have surfaced. This is not to fashion a silk purse from a pig's ear, but rather to understand that in the course of living, the tough moments can become the best. They help to secure the value proposition.

◆ ◆ ◆

Following layoffs at Tyndale during 1995–1996, there was deep anger and hurt over what had happened and how staff and faculty had been treated. I knew we needed to find a means of releasing those emotions, bringing closure to those deep feelings.

We took an Old Testament model of priests who took a goat and, after symbolically loading the sins of the people onto its back, sent it into the wilderness to die. I wrote a liturgy for a public service we called The Solemn Assembly, including prayers for our sins, declaring our trust in God, and providing a means to release sorrow, fear, and anger.

The service concluded with handing out slips of paper on which participants were to write what issues they were prepared to release to the Lord. We placed a large pot with a burning candle at the front of the chapel. I invited those who wanted to release their hurts, fears, and anger to come to the front and allow the fire to burn their confessional release, trusting the Spirit to lift their burdens.

I had no idea who would respond. At the invitation, a line formed. Most attendees joined in. I wondered why the line moved so slowly. Then I saw that as faculty and staff dropped their confessional releases onto the flame, they didn't walk away but stood there, watching until the paper was consumed.

It was a critical turning point, a clearing of inner issues that we dared not overlook or allow to pass by. The crisis became a teacher, reminding us of our life of faith: forgiveness of others and the Father's forgiveness of us. It was a means of securing in our community of faith our essential value proposition.

◆ ◆ ◆

The following steps are helpful in understanding and utilizing a crisis.

IDENTIFY THE ESSENTIAL AND VALUABLE RESOURCES RESIDENT IN THE ENTERPRISE

In my early days with the Evangelical Fellowship of Canada, I knew that even though it had been started for good reason, it had not moved beyond its early start apart from a few conferences.

As I examined the survey we had done on Canadian evangelicals' concerns, I saw Canadians looking for answers to social and ethical questions, and I recognized the potential of creating a national identity for three million evangelicals. We had little money (about $25,000 a year), no administrative base, and no full-time staff. The only means of communication was a quarterly magazine called *Thrust*.

The essential and valuable resources were the name and nature of organization. Within a community of fifty denominations, the EFC was the center around which evangelical denominations, parachurch ministries, educational communities, and missions could gather. Here was our opportunity. What was needed was a functioning organization and a public voice that spoke with reason and conviction.

IDENTIFY PARTS OF THE ORGANIZATION THAT NEED TO BE LAID ASIDE

We knew we needed a strong, national communication piece—in days before the Internet—one that spoke to our concerns and informed our community of what was going on in the nation. The old magazine had to go. We rebuilt with a new magazine, *Faith Today*.

We also laid aside two constraining attitudes and policies. In the U.S., the National Association of Evangelicals (NAE) had a rule that didn't allow church groups to belong to both the National Council of Churches (mainline denominations) and the NAE. We decided it was none of our business what other organizations a member of the EFC belonged to. We agreed that our tent would be wide.

Also, it was apparent that traditional evangelical antipathy to the Roman Catholic Church was counterproductive. In Canada, the Catholic community comprises over 40 percent of the population, making it the largest church in Canada and of enormous influence. On major ethical and social issues we had more of a consensus with Roman Catholics than with mainline Protestants. This relationship was productive in engagement on political and legal matters and it took the sharp edge off the reputation we had gained as reactionary and strident. This opened a new and fruitful friendship and allowed for cooperative strategies.

IDENTIFY WHY IT IS IMPORTANT TO CONTINUE THE WORK AND THUS CAUSE A RELAUNCH

To ask it another way, apart from nostalgia and lingering interests of long-time members, are there reasons that others would want to invest in rebuilding? You may think it a wonderful idea, but does anyone else?

Tyndale's financial dilemma became an opportunity for the solution of one of its core challenges, which was that undergraduate Christian education was changing. As noted earlier, the paradigm of Christian education—

Christian high school grads taking a few years of Bible college for spiritual preparation before they set out on their vocational prep—was becoming unworkable. While students still wanted to learn the Scriptures and be grounded in faith, they also wanted an education with recognized degrees that employers other than churches and religious institutions would regard. In the mid 1990s students were voting with their feet.

This economic disaster of a declining enrolment helped us identify our value proposition, which in turn provided the opportunity to turn the college into a university, retain the essence of its former life, and broaden it into a new, more creative, and desired form of Christian education. Without the crisis, the transition would have been more difficult.

PRINCIPLE 5

Bridge the Dialectic of Passion and Planning

Write it down. Written goals have a way of transforming wishes into wants; cant's into cans; dreams into plans; and plans into reality. Don't just think it; ink it!

—Author Unknown

A schedule defends from chaos and whim. It is a net for catching days. It is scaffolding on which a worker can stand and labor with both hands at sections of time.

—Annie Dillard

To a visionary, fueled by the possibility of faith in action, planning sounds almost like "unfaith," as if thinking about the steps in making the vision a reality is a sort of doubt.

IMPORTANCE OF STRATEGIC PLANNING

Being able to see from 33,000 feet has its problems, as I've often learned. From that vantage point I'm able to describe the vision, what will be in five years. The story of what has been, what is, and what will be plays like a well-rehearsed concerto. What I struggle with is breaking it down into steps, getting from here to there.

Often, in articulating a vision I knew the broad strokes of strategy, but knowing that only complicated it for others. The strategy wasn't sufficiently detailed for the team who had to manage it to fulfillment.

FIND A BROKEN WALL

As I pointed out in the previous chapter, in my last years as president of
YFC, I confused my senior team with ideas that made perfect sense to me,
but because they hadn't been agreed on and connected to the vision and
mission, I was out on my own. Senior staff assumed I had lost interest in
the work. In a way they were right—I was tired with the role and with
being unable to mobilize the team to growth. But rather than work with
them in developing a strategy, I created new plans and developed new
teams. This led to a misunderstanding. How much better it would have
been if I had been disciplined to develop a working plan that had everyone
onside.

Fixing broken ministries requires more than passion. Coordinating volunteers, protecting them from enemies, encouraging them to keep going in
the face of danger requires passion. Hearts filled with a desire to see the
project finished are essential to the strategy. But it takes more than that.

Important ideas become reality when a plan is designed and carried out.
The building of a major work takes years in the planning, as North
Americans learned from the Japanese. Someone noted, "It takes the
Japanese ten years to plan and one year to implement; North Americans
take one year in planning and ten in implementation."

Passion without planning leads to chaos. Montreal's Expo '67, Man and
His World, was a marvelous event, but lack of preparation resulted in a
massive overrun of costs in a driving urgency to get it done on time. The
enormous debt, which required the province of Quebec to levy an extra
property tax, took four decades to pay off.

As passionate as you are, your vision and need for activity must not keep
you from putting in place a strategic plan—or at least appointing someone
(from within or from the outside) to help you.

A romantic read of Nehemiah overlooks the impact of his planning and
forethought. Overcome by the force of his vision, we might ignore the
deliberate and progressive ingredients of his planning and execution.
Nehemiah had to convince the most powerful leader on earth to buy into
his idea. Such persuasion required him to have a plan. Notice what he
identified and the steps he took:

1. He convinced the king to allow him to return to Jerusalem. His presentation would have been filled with passion and color. Vision played into

102

the story he told. Even so, it was a careful step, located in a plan. This first step was necessary, for only then could he proceed to the next.

2. He worked out sufficient detail to persuade the king to provide financial support. Such a king wouldn't risk international conflict simply on a well-told story. The king needed to see that the project was doable and that Nehemiah had sufficient understanding of what it took to get it done.

3. Nehemiah had the foresight to get letters of introduction for both safe passage and acquisition of building materials. Paperwork! The bane of visionaries. Great ideas described with great passion and conviction fall to the floor over a failure to do the groundwork. I know, for there have been too many such ideas in my life for me to ignore.

4. Then he made a deal with Asaph for lumber. It was possible because he had requested an introduction. Bluster wouldn't work. As powerful as Nehemiah was within his own regime, he understood politics. He knew the critical nature of having the king open the door. That took planning. (Later in the book, I'll address the politics of operation.)

5. If Nehemiah had arrived in Jerusalem without the necessary resources, all the great speeches in the world would not have overcome the need for lumber. An estimate of what was needed allowed him to gather supplies so that when it was time to go to work they had what was needed.

6. He needed authority, so he asked to be called governor of Judah. This critical position gave him leverage to deal with a debilitating problem of the poor being charged high interest. His forethought kept him from being hemmed in by the social and political dynamics of the complex world of Jerusalem.

7. It took more than enthusiasm to get the Jerusalem Jews into action. They needed to be organized. Collecting people with passion for the project required plans.

WHAT IS STRATEGIC PLANNING?

Strategic planning is more than writing out a strategy and listing the ingredients required. It is first about thinking—thinking what is, what needs to be, what can be done, and ways it can be accomplished. It starts with thinking about the bigger picture.

Nick Carter, of Andover Newton Seminary, says that strategic planning falls into three categories: problem planning, long-range planning, and transformative planning. All three have value. However, here I want us to understand transformative planning: a process that transforms what is, to rebuild the broken.

In his book *Unfunded: From Bootstrap to Blue Chip, Starting a Fire without the Fuel of Round-A Capital*, Carter suggests four important considerations in strategic planning:

1. Each business, organization, and agency has its own history, ethos, and community. Strategic planning formats are many. Carefully determine what is appropriate for your setting.

2. The vitality of your organization depends on you, the leader, to think and lead strategically and to create energy in planning strategically with others.

3. Your vision comes from within, not without. It cannot be imposed.

4. Strategic planning will, in the end, be one of the most important initiatives you will lead.

WHAT IS THE VALUE OF A STRATEGIC PLAN?

It brings vision from 33,000 feet to ground level.

Visionaries by nature visualize the project completed but might find it difficult to describe its elements. Calling on the visionary to be more specific presses him or her to unwrap the ideas with more specificity. It forces vision to be broken up into bite-sized chunks.

It helps demonstrate the vision's workability and possibility.

How many ideas find their way into reality? Inventors try and try and, after scores of attempts, see only a low percentage of ideas actually take off. Ministries that deal in the less-than-quantifiable world of spiritual well-being have greater difficulty in achieving concrete results than a business. That makes it even more important to work at identifying the plan.

It shows the weaknesses of the organization and what is needed to complement its operation.

Fearful of opposition, a visionary may believe there are no weaknesses or that identifying them will unravel the vision. The better an idea is refined, the greater the possibility of success.

It engages the community in thinking about what is envisioned and how it may be accomplished.

Visionaries tend to be proprietary with their ideas, protecting them within boundaries of their own interest. Planning presses them out of such limiting emotions and, by drawing in the community, improves and expands the idea.

It identifies the important ingredients needed for fulfilling the project.

Before Nehemiah set out for Jerusalem, his planning forced him to identify what was needed. That brought him face to face with the political dynamics of the region and prepared him for their inevitable impact on the project.

It brings major parties into play, calling on their visions, gifts, and adaptability.

In recruiting, help people visualize where they fit. A plan identifies the places that need to be filled. Most people know instinctively what they do best, but self-selection works only if the plan has sufficient details.

Some stakeholders contribute financially, but for most people, time is the larger contribution. In a busy world of demands, participants will need to see where their gifts and schedules fit into the vision. With a plan, the vision will more likely attract the needed skills.

It lays out a schedule that motivates and disciplines those involved.

In molding a team, a plan helps each one know what is expected.

It monitors accountability.

In working with volunteers, accountability becomes a serious part of compensation. It works this way: if the leader takes time to review the work of the volunteer, it is a clear message to the volunteer that his or her contribution is worth the leader's time. This heightens their sense of worth.

Accountability is equally important for staff, however. It demonstrates that they and the quality of their work are important to the organization.

Accountability happens, though, only when there are agreed-on markers of accomplishment and diligence.

WHAT DOES IT TAKE TO COMPLETE A STRATEGIC PLAN?

Someone to take charge

A strategic plan helps to ensure the success of an organization. When people see the value of the plan, they will instinctively promote its importance, subject themselves to its discipline, and serve the person who oversees it.

There is great value in assigning someone to oversee the development and implementation of a strategic plan. Recruit someone you trust to do what you can't do.

Adaptability

Developing a strategic plan does not imply that the course ahead is fixed. Who can predict the next twelve months, let alone three or five years?

Assumptions of adaptability—willingness and ability to quickly shift gears and rework the plan—are innate to strategic planning. In *Leadership without Easy Answers,* Ron Heifetz, director of the Leadership Education Project, notes that in being *adaptive,* one considers not only the values that the goal represents, but also the goal's ability to mobilize people to face, rather than avoid, tough realities and conflicts. The hardest and most valuable task of leadership may be advancing goals and designing strategies that promote adaptive work."

Adaptability calls for an examination of what is being done during the process, not just what has been done on completion. By avoiding the temptation to let the end justify the means, the means is given due consideration as critical in testing the value of the end.

WHERE DOES ONE BEGIN?

Take time. Allow for research, assessment, and planning before beginning. Make an environmental assessment of your organization and your world.

The SWOT system is a good place to begin:

Strengths

Weaknesses

Opportunities

Threats

Bring together internal and external parties and brainstorm each category. Write lists on large sheets of paper and post them around the room. Then go back over the process to see what you've missed and what should be eliminated. This will give you a view of the environment and point out aspects you possibly had not thought of. Allow this to gestate. A few weeks later, revisit the process to refine the lists and your understanding of the environment and project.

Above all, make everyone a part of the process. Give team members a sense of ownership as they better understand that their ideas matter.

Link into outside contributors. I was speaking at a seminary on the topic of leadership, and after a day I felt boxed in. Reflecting, I realized everything during that day—conversations, lectures, papers, debates—reflected the assumption that the school's particular denomination was the only Christian community on the planet. My attempts to help them see from outside got nowhere. Their interest was locked into their own tribal concerns. Get outside people to not only help you "think outside the box" but "live outside the box."

As you begin, consider this framework for planning:

1. Research, reflect, and review the context of planning. Give yourself time to think about the world in which you live and serve. It is in constant change, requiring reflection on the nature, cause, and speed of change.

2. Review and reflect on your ethos, disposition, or characteristic spirit. We grow from our roots, a history that contributes to who we now are. Ask what your group assumes is true, good, and worthwhile out of that history.

3. Research for the process that best suits your needs. Formulas aren't sacred. Some people will have their pet schematics. Don't be trapped. Have a specialist help you look at your group and advise you.

4. Keep yourself, as leader, free to intellectually roam the ideas without having to own what is percolating or having to supervise the meetings. Find someone else to chair. Bring in an outsider who is professional enough to handle any discordant views that may surface.

WHAT DOES A STRATEGIC PLAN LOOK LIKE IN REAL LIFE?

The GOST outline (Goal, Objective, Strategy, and Tactic, explained by leadership coach Bob Gernon in *Body and Soul: Unleashing the Power of Your Team*) provides a framework in designating responsibility. It is made up of four primary building blocks:

Goal(s): the primary aim of the vision

Objectives: specific elements required to achieve the goal

Strategy: the way it will be done

Tactics: specific steps to take

NEHEMIAH'S STRATEGIC PLAN

To see what this looks like in life, let's apply the GOST format to Nehemiah. Though we are looking at it from the outside, we can imagine what he was doing in the early days of organizing the rebuilding.

In this case, his single goal was to renew the people of God. Building the wall was not even an objective but a strategy.

Goal = I.

    Objective = a.

        Strategy = i.

            Tactic = 1.

I. To renew the People of God

    a. To secure the Temple

        i. Get the king of Persia on side.

            1. Convince the king of the strategic importance of rebuilding the Jerusalem wall.

2. Convince him to give Nehemiah a leave of absence.

3. Get letters from him, ensuring his continuing support.

ii. Recruit resources.

1. Have in hand a letter of introduction to suppliers.

2. Ensure there is sufficient protection for personnel and supplies

iii. Motivate Jews of Jerusalem for the project.

1. Be well informed first of the need.

2. Convince them of the need to act now.

3. Show them it can be done.

4. Help them see God is with them.

5. Give evidence that needed material is available.

iv. Rebuild the wall.

1. Identify the specific need.

2. Draft a plan for the wall.

3. Show how it can be done.

4. Cultivate trust with the influentials in Jerusalem.

5. Mobilize the workforce.

6. Build in accountability.

7. Arrange for protection.

v. Shut down opposition.

1. Handle the ridicule.

2. Consolidate the opposing forces into a plan for response.

3. Neutralize intimidation.

4. Give evidence of the king's support.

b. **Restore the well-being of Jews in the region.**

    i. Ensure that the Jerusalem Jews know that rebuilding the wall is part of God's agenda.

        1. *Outline the many ways the plans have begun to come together.*

        2. *Point out the importance of the Temple and the need to protect the rebuilding of the wall.*

        3. *Recruit workers, keeping in mind that the most successful searches come by active recruitment.*

    ii. Use authority as governor.

        1. *Build credibility: don't take payment, though it is rightful to accept.*

        2. *Be visible in every part of the rebuilding.*

        3. *Determine the role of governor.*

    iii. Demonstrate how authority helps their well-being.

        1. *Show workers your plan to protect them from enemies.*

        2. *Oversee complaints of unfairness.*

        3. *Create a fair policy for use and processing of monies.*

    iv. Dedicate the wall.

        1. *Make it memorable.*

        2. *Use music.*

c. **Establish Israel as a home for Jewish people.**

    i. Identify those who have legitimate claims to Jerusalem.

        1. *Register those with proof of ancestry.*

        2. *Make plans for those living outside the walls.*

    ii. Identify role of the Temple.

        1. *Make plans for public confession and worship.*

2. Organize music celebration.

3. Prepare to introduce people to their story of faith.

4. Arrange for the priest to attend and read the Law of Moses.

iii. Recruit religious leadership to serve in worship at the Temple.

1. Identify priests.

2. Identify Levites.

d. **Write laws to organize and guide Jews now living in Jerusalem.**

i. Ensure that the Law of Moses is read and understood.

1. Set in place a permanent priest who is financed.

2. Arrange for Levites to be financed.

ii. Structure society so it has means of judging those accused of misadventure.

1. Set in place judges to supervise the upholding of the law.

Note that Nehemiah had one goal: not to rebuild the walls but to renew the people of God. Rebuilding was a strategy.

Nehemiah's challenge was to help the Jewish people regain their place as God's light to the world. Rebuilding—as a strategy—served the goal, the bigger reality. We are tempted to make strategy a goal. If Nehemiah had seen rebuilding the wall as the goal, he would have lost sight of the other factors that flowed from the real goal: to renew the people of God in their faith.

TYNDALE'S STRATEGIC PLAN

At Tyndale we had three objectives. First to survive—if the school had shut down that first summer, the likelihood of restarting was nil. We had sixty days to get it up and running for the fall semester. The second was to re-create—this over-a-century-old college needed an overhaul. The third was to build sustainability.

Though the troubles of Tyndale were financial shortages, the underlying issue was financial management.

As a new team took hold, costs had to be curtailed and revenue increased. Through the first couple of years we did mainly operational corrections just to get functioning. The redevelopment of the board was strategic in establishing corporate authority and governance.

Even so, strategic issues were at the heart of our considerations. While we kept to the operational matters and let our community know what we were doing to fix the immediate issues, long were our conversations with the board, senior staff, faculty, and key donors on strategic matters.

WHAT DOES STRATEGIC PLANNING REQUIRE?

Strategic planning requires thinking. Think about what it is you are thinking about.

It is one thing to think about what needs to be done but another to think about what you are thinking of doing. You may imagine planting a new church or taking on a broken-down organization or business. That is what you are thinking about. Now lift that to another level and ask, What am I thinking about as I go about doing?

In rebuilding Tyndale, the immediate issue was to get it up and running so it wouldn't lose a semester. Not only did we think about getting sufficient monies in the first summer, we focused on details in making it work. But rebuilding was more than making the school operational that fall; it was about thinking what this educational community was. Why did it exist? Was there a common world where others had knowledge about what we were doing? Did we know those people? Could we work together?

In *Leadership, New and Revised*, Peter Koestenbaum identifies ten critical points around which rebuilding would be helped by thinking about what we are doing.

1. Leadership is about achieving results. Those in a church-related world are prone to couch "results" within spiritual metaphors that may end up in obscuring the leader's role. Acting Christianly with a servant attitude is important, but don't let it obscure your role in reaching objectives.

2. Leading is about influencing how people think. Linking activity with good habits and practice ingrains into people that which will serve them in difficult times.

3. Be willing to change: allow the moment to infuse you with new ideas and press you to consider new models. Admit that some things are being done wrong or are no longer needed. Push past the status quo, past the human inclination to stay where you are, refusing the slippery slope of trying harder to do the same things you've done in the past.

4. Strengthen your understanding by teaching it to others. As you hear yourself teach it to others, it acts as a check and reinforcement. When we reflect on the what and how of our work, we become more conscious of what we do either reflectively or intuitively.

5. Learn by doing. "What they didn't teach me at Harvard" wasn't a put-down of the educational offerings or that of any other school. It simply was a reminder that our primary way of learning is by doing. Courses and books on leadership will help in framing the questions and advising what one might expect, but the place we do our best learning is in the laboratory of leading. Mistakes, fair game for us all, are essential in the learning process. This is not an excuse but an understanding that the critical lessons of life are discovered in the doing.

6. Learn to live with ambiguity. Much of life is lived in the gray zones. Though people need direction from their leader, within the group there will be varying points of view. People see things differently. Differing views may be valid and may be held by wise and trustworthy people. Hold them together like an orchestra, as Koestenbaum suggests, bringing various tones and parts into harmony.

7. Be faithful in nurturing the important areas of life: employment, family, self-development, spirituality, economic well-being. For example, be careful that in your focus on ministry and enterprise, your sense of self-giving doesn't cloud family needs.

8. In the daily life of your ministry, build in teachable elements of what serving looks like. By so doing you add value to your staff and community.

9. Learn from other models and people. Trees grow naturally, but in our yard they grow according to what my pruning allows. I determine how they will be shaped. They do the growing; I do the shaping. And I do so from what I see arborists do.

10. Expect that what you do will enhance those in the organization and community. Have it in your mind to say when you leave, "It is in better

shape than when I came." There will be days when a misadventure, a wrong word, or something over which you had no control will create a reversal, and you will despair of moving forward. Keep at it. Stay with the essentials.

◆ ◆ ◆

Developing a strategy is not simply a matter of writing it out. It comes from struggle, trial, and mistakes. At Tyndale we developed an understanding of what was needed as we progressed. Let me first note the nature of the broken wall at Tyndale and how we began to rebuild it.

When I took on this challenge, I had no idea how badly broken were the walls. Before I agreed to help, I asked my brother Dave his opinion. Because of his experience in business and management I respected and trusted his wise counsel.

After some days on campus he had a grasp of the true picture: the debt was $6 million, and assets (determined on a "distress sale" basis) were worth about $4.5 million. The accumulated deficits of the schools had snowballed to insolvency.

How had all this come to pass?

One cause was the widening gap between expenses and income. Another was the school's borrowing of restricted funds—dedicated for scholarships and bursaries—to pay for operations. This created a false economy and false sense of economic stability. A third factor was the building of a seminary facility. Pledges had been made, but the recession of the early 1990s had calamitous effects, and a percentage of the pledges never materialized. Some donors had given for a designated investment. When the investment was lost in the insolvency I met with each person, one on one, outlining the issue and what we believed was the way forward.

Immediately three of us came together to forge a fund-raising plan: Steve Hubley, a marketing manager with whom I had worked, and Larry Willard, a seminary grad with skills and experience in marketing, and me. We called it Operation Restore. We told the story as plainly and clearly as we could. We agreed that we would be up front with details, without casting aspersions, and update supporters often on what was needed, the results of new initiatives, and the next issue that needed solving. Within weeks, the school community responded. By the end of August we had enough money to reopen for the fall semester.

At the time we were at a critical juncture with the creditors. The trustee under whose authority the government allowed us to operate was helping us design a proposal to the creditors. If they accepted it, we could move forward. If they voted no, then at that very moment we would fall into bankruptcy, lose our charitable status, and be wound up as an organization. The date for the meeting of the creditors was November 7, 1995, at which time they would vote on our proposal. Almost 100 percent of creditors approved, and we moved forward. We implemented our plan and in time paid off our creditors, re-established good faith with our bankers, and gradually implemented a long-term strategy of growth. Winston Ling, a retired executive from corporate leadership, then took hold of finances and over the coming years became a trusted and indispensable partner.

Planning is to vision what wheels are to a motor. Gusto, power, and potential are essential to moving forward, but without wheels all you get is a roar.

The discipline of planning is a vital bridging of the opposites of vision and implementation. Your determination to do good strategic planning will not only enhance the vision but move it into reality. Think of it as your most important initiative as leader.

PRINCIPLE 6

Recognize that Recruiting Resources Is a Litmus Test of Leadership

Throw your net on the right side of the boat.

—Jesus, John 21:6

If you want to build a ship, don't drum up the men to gather wood, divide the work, and give orders. Instead teach them to yearn for the vast and endless sea.

—Antoine de Saint-Exupéry

Leaders instinctively recruit resources in accomplishing their mission. Those who don't, are reluctant to, or can't are not what we understand to be leaders.

While that may sound tough, if you haven't figured out that building resources is central to your calling as leader, you may misunderstand the nature of leadership. If you are responsible for recruiting a leader and if you modify the definition, making allowances for a candidate with, "Well, I'm sure we'll get the needed support some way," you are courting disaster.

For Nehemiah, resource development began in his first conversation with the king. No sooner had the king agreed, than Nehemiah asked,

> "If it pleases the king, may I have letters to the governors of Tran-Euphrates, so that they will provide me safe-conduct until I arrive in Judah? And may I have a letter to Asaph, keeper of the king's forest, so he will give me timber to make beams for the gates of the

citadel by the temple and for the city wall and for the residence I will occupy?" (Nehemiah 2:7, 8)

Don't separate vision from sustainability. If an undertaking is worth the start, it is worth the finish.

Money, a creation gift, is integral to all of life. If leaders exclude resources in their equation, it is a sure sign something is wrong. Even so, many organizations are inclined to leave it on the bottom rung of priorities, rather than lifting it to the top, ensuring the venture has the resources to succeed.

Learn from Nehemiah.

THE IMPORTANCE OF GIVING

TREASURE FOLLOWS THE HEART

Money is a critical means by which humans interact, a fundamental ingredient without which societies would grind to a halt. Jesus spoke often about money, factoring it into the heart of his calling.

I saw this issue differently when I discovered that I had misunderstood a biblical insight.

In the Beatitudes Jesus said,

> "Do not store up for yourselves treasures on earth, where moth and rust destroy, and where thieves break in and steal.
>
> But store up for yourselves treasures in heaven, where moth and rust do not destroy, and where thieves do not break in and steal.
>
> For where your treasure is, there your heart will be also." (Matthew 6:19–21)

There it is. That last line: "For where your *treasure* is, there your *heart* will be also."

I assumed it meant, "For where your *heart* is, there your *treasure* will be also."

I had inverted "heart" and "treasure" for a natural reason: my heart attracts my wallet. When I'm emotionally moved, I give. Many organizations working with the poor, broken, and underprivileged play that heartstring in fund-raising.

But that's not what Jesus said. Though he didn't say emotions are not a trigger point in giving, in this text, he spoke about ownership and investment.

So what was he saying? Giving links a person's interest. Investment transforms the heart.

In our devotions, Lily and I instinctively recall those we financially support. Giving to people, organizations, and missions compels our interest. For good reason: our investment locates our interest in wanting to know their needs, interests, and work. The gift secures our interest.

Think in terms of a financial portfolio. When you own a stock, you notice its rise and fall more so than stocks in which you have no investment. In giving to the cancer society, you develop a better understanding of the disease, are more attentive to new discoveries, and are more inclined to sign up as a volunteer. Why? Your treasure secured your heart.

As president of Tyndale, my task was to engage people with the enterprise. To do that, I became part of the stewardship program, knowing that giving pulled donors' interest into Tyndale's mission and strategy.

Pastor, who are your most faithful members? Not surprising, those who give regularly. An important lesson to teach your people is the benefit of faithful giving. Wonder why congregants wander around from church to church? Music perhaps. Better youth resources as well. However, the hearts of those who give will be anchored, and the comings and goings of styles and worship music will be less likely to draw them away. Cynical and undisciplined people are less likely to be consistent in giving. Money links our hearts to the cause, be it Jesus or cancer research. It is a life principle that crosses all boundaries.

GIFTS BECOME LEVERS OF ENCOURAGEMENT AND ACCELERATION

Small and large gifts influence the well-being of the ministry. During the first summer of trying to right the Tyndale schools and get them opened for the fall, we came to the deadline of our donation drive to meet our immediate needs. We were short $40,000.

Larry Willard and David Stiller were in the Tyndale coffee shop near the college entrance when a lady walked in and, in halting English, asked to see someone about making a gift. She had received an inheritance from a relative in Hong Kong and chose to make a gift to Tyndale.

On that last day of the campaign, a person led by the Spirit gave a gift of the exact amount needed. Imagine the ripple effect that had. If we ever believed the schools could be rescued, it was that day.

GIVING ACCOMPLISHES WHAT DONORS CAN'T DO ON THEIR OWN

One day I received a letter from a donor who had a half million dollars to give to Tyndale. Some weeks later, I spent an afternoon with her and her husband, getting to know them, hearing their combined story of faith. Over the years, she had carefully saved from the couple's modest income.

I asked why she wanted to give her savings to Tyndale. "Because you will know what to do with it," she said resolutely.

On the way out I said, "You look so happy now."

"Yes," she replied, "the money is now in your hands."

I understood. She had a heart for training young people, but it was something she could not do on her own. In trusting us with her funds, she extended her life so that with us, she could do what she wanted to accomplish.

Not surprisingly, we speak of *trust* in handling money. People trust leaders, and when they give to organizations they do so believing the funds will be used to fulfill their own passion and accomplish what we promised. We become the means by which people's accumulated savings extend their lives into ministry. We hold living legacies from their years of working. As leaders, we have the privilege of entering into people's lives by offering a conduit of service in a way that is consistent with their giving, praying, and serving.

To say it another way, people need us to carry on their testimony. Increasingly parents recognize that leaving too much money to their children and grandchildren can be self-defeating. Many are the stories of how a large inheritance can destroy an heir's will to work, to be responsible, to be personally motivated and to have inner discipline.

FUND-RAISING AS ESSENTIAL TO LEADERSHIP

Let's connect the dots: leaders bring people together around a mission. Giving is a means of testing followership. As we capture supporters' giving, we capture their hearts.

Before we go further, understand what I mean by leadership. We loosely use the word to describe image makers, idea formulators, spokespeople, promoters, philosophers, pundits, and advocates who influence people, ideas, and products. In a general sense such people lead in that they influence by their ideas or personality. That's not what I mean by leading.

I have in mind those who actually head up movements, organizations, business, missions, and congregations—in short, those who, in exercising authority, guide others in doing good. In that position, leaders are responsible to see that resources are recruited to fulfill the mission.

If you don't, are unwilling to, or deem yourself unable to see that resources are recruited, then by definition you aren't leading.

Raising funds is not only a high priority for a leader, it is a wonderful calling. I find that it connects me in a more personal way to people as I spend time with them and learn of their families, aspirations, needs, and opportunities. Then I find ways to serve: sending books, attending weddings and funerals, grieving in times of sorrow, and praying in moments of decision-making.

FUND-RAISING IS ABOUT HEART TRANSFORMATION

Leaders seek human transformation. It doesn't happen immediately. It takes time. It requires nurturing and building relationships.

Don't assume that making people feel good will result in support. It's important to create good will. Good feelings always make the process easier. However, getting people to feel good about your ministry or project doesn't automatically translate into giving. Giving is a transaction in which the case for support is made and the request to participate is clearly presented, then followed up on. That is the beginning of what might very well be a long relationship that will hopefully transform a potential donor into a supporter with a heart for your mission.

In the beginnings of the EFC, our donation budget was very modest. A decade and a half later it had grown to several million dollars. When I left

I was pleased to hear investors say, "We began giving when you challenged us, and we want you to know now that even though you are leaving, we will continue our support." Their hearts were fused into the mission and vision by their investments.

Leaders by nature attract people to their mission. How do you know if you are a leader? By those who join in your vision. And how will you know if people have really joined? When their hearts are linked with yours. And how will you know that? By their giving.

What principle is at work here?

Jesus invites us to view treasure differently: when you invest, your heart will be linked to its cause and calling.

Fund-raising is about heart transformation. Convince someone of a good place to invest, and the person's heart will be changed.

COMMON OBJECTIONS FROM LEADERS

I know some people will react negatively to including recruiting resources as an essential role of leadership. I hear various excuses for not engaging in fund-raising.

I don't have what it takes to be a fund-raiser.

It may be you are reacting to a caricature, someone who has been offensive, insensitive, or smooth. Don't allow stereotypes to hold you back.

I want for you as leader a life-altering perspective that will set your leadership free in new, creative, and powerful ways.

I don't like it.

So? I don't like to do detailed reports. Many things we don't enjoy, but they need doing.

I'll get others to do it.

Of course you will. Depending on the size of the organization, others will help. But prime benefactors will want to hear from you, to hear *you* describe the vision and to sense your passion.

I've more important things to do.

Not really. In a start-up, you will juggle many tasks, one being to speak of your mission and vision. When payday comes and there's a lack of money, it is the leader that people look to for a solution. Better to have thought of that long before that day.

A mission worth doing needs to be sustained. Regardless of the vision's importance or necessity, it will end as mere words if building a support base hasn't been essential to your life and schedule.

People don't like me speaking of money.

I've found that isn't true. We assembled 2,500 donor names from four mission organizations and hired a research company to ask a series of questions focused around attitudes of money. People who gave to these agencies said their number one request of their pastor was to help them manage money. An understanding of giving is as natural to the managing of money as seeding is to the process of farming.

Some fund-raisers make me bristle.

Join the line. Organizations make a mistake by turning the raising of funds over to those who are able to pitch the request but lack credibility, or who sound like an infomercial selling salad-cutters or rotisseries.

However, because others have done it poorly is no reason not to do it at all.

Some people are turned off when I ask them to help.

As I recall, I've been turned down sharply by no more than ten people in almost five decades of making thousands of request for funds. If the case statement is clear and compelling, if the setting in which the request is being made is appropriate, and if a simple invitation is made, people are willing, and indeed honored, to be invited.

People aren't interested.

How do you know? Has it been tested? If so, by whom—an independent researcher who knows how to ask good questions that lead to honest and helpful answers? If you are interested, you can interest others.

There are not enough resources out there.

Resources are not zero-sum. In many parts of the world, resources are available for a compelling cause. Just because someone gives to one cause doesn't mean she or he won't have resources for another. Terry Winter, a former national television host, and I had worked together in a variety of causes. Early in our friendship we collaborated on our plans and willingly introduced each other to donors.

If any one or a combination of these objections slows you down, it may show that you lack ability to lead. Leadership requires that the securing of resources be front and center in what we do.

REASONS WHY RAISING RESOURCES IS A LITMUS TEST

Why is raising resources a litmus test for leadership? Let me offer some reasons.

A leader articulates the mission.

Volunteers, donors, associates, and the public need to hear *you* outline the vision and sense your passion. Moses protested, pleading lack of skill, and his brother, Aaron, stood in. But when they got going, Moses was the leader the people heard. You may need to work on your presentation skills, but don't allow anxiety to keep you from outlining where you are going and what it will take to get there.

Tell people often what you plan to do and when. In the early days at Tyndale and for the following decade and half, I spoke again and again of our mission: to build a great center for Christian higher education in Toronto, North America's fourth largest city. It was here I dreamed not only about what would be but the "what ifs." People are interested in what you visualize for the coming years.

A leader draws hearts to the mission.

I said it earlier: resources define those who are committed to the mission. As the leader wins hearts, resources given become part of the exchange.

BENEFITS OF THE LEADER BEING INVOLVED IN FUND-RAISING

I've explained that, strategically, it matters that resource generation be among your highest priorities. There are other, more personal reasons why it is critical for you to be party to donor development.

1. It is personally renewing.

Donor development is similar to other kinds of visits. You come face to face with another person's needs, issues, and concerns. It gives you opportunity to speak hope and love into that life and leave knowing you've been a contributor.

2. You may have existing connections.

You may already be building relationships with people who can help you in your mission. Is it manipulation to ask a friend for support?

How you handle it is the point. Recruiting resources is not manipulating friendship to get your way. First it might be helpful—if you are dealing with a close friend or relative—to remind the person that you have a role as leader to fill. Ask, "Could I take a few minutes and tell you about what is going on, and would you be open to me laying before you possible opportunities of being involved?" It is wise to ask permission.

3. You are personally invested.

I assume you are making significant personal sacrifice in your own giving to support the cause. Don't fall into the trap of convincing yourself that your time or low salary is your contribution. When asked to support a campaign or annual fund, I ask the leader how much she or he is giving. With both your heart and finances invested, you have moral ground to stand on.

◆ ◆ ◆

During the development of Tyndale's major financial campaign—with a goal larger than that of any religious group in Canada's history at the time—Lily and I agreed to give an amount larger than we had ever given. We believed it was important to set the pattern by our giving.

Friend and mentor Henry Wildeboer probed my giving to the capital campaign by bluntly asking how much we were giving. I answered, thinking the amount would impress him. "Was it sacrificial?" he asked.

What a question! It had not been that difficult, because of a successful investment and a recent Canadian tax law. Some days later I told Lily of the conversation. As the one who looks after our household accounts, she knew exactly what we could afford. She asked what I thought we should do. Hesitantly I gave her a number close to that of our annual income.

In time we agreed we would trust the Lord for that amount. We didn't have it, and we still had an outstanding debt and personal commitment.

We learned the lesson of faith and the importance of doing what we asked others to do. Within fewer years than we expected, we happily moved along in meeting our commitment.

◆ ◆ ◆

4. It keeps you in touch with a broader reality.

For years my scheduling rule has been to have three donor appointments a week. This discipline moves me out of the office to engage with others. As much as vision is exciting and renewing, it must be actualized in the schedule. Here is where you win or lose: what does your calendar show for next week? If meeting with donors hasn't been arranged, it won't happen. The common default in a leader's life is to allow administrative detail to block out fund development, a default that calls for deliberate resistance. Embed in your plans times of meeting with people other than those in the organization.

As you get off your island, you will speak language other than the jargon of your community. When working with youth I learned to speak about faith in non-religious language. If I didn't, I'd lose the audience.

I asked the senior minister in a Chinese church, "How many attending this service understand English?" Earlier that Sunday morning I had spoken to the English service; the second was in the Cantonese language, and I spoke with an interpreter.

He replied, "About 95 percent."

"So why don't they come to the English service?"

"There is no echo."

"Echo?" Then I understood: most of the people spoke English in their work, but as it wasn't their first language, they would mentally translate it to their native tongue. Hearing the message and singing hymns in their home language allowed the ideas to echo in their mind. Words, music, intonation all connect to memories and experiences, reinforcing and clarifying ideas.

By sitting in a donor's world, your language, metaphors, and ideas will echo.

5. You will be stretched.

Many donors you deal with will be professional people or entrepreneurs who know the importance of risk and inventiveness and the dangers of the status quo. Meeting such people can be a risk. They may press you to options that cause you discomfort.

An enormous benefit of meeting with donors is that it encourages you to live beyond the fences of former years. In conversing with donors, you will realize that the "same old" will not capture or sustain interest.

6. It inspires your staff.

As CEO or president, you demonstrate to staff the importance of the mission as they see your passion and commitment in meeting donors and building resources.

It also spreads the story. Take a member of the staff or the board with you on donor visits so they will better understand the importance of donor development.

7. Investors want to hear from the leader.

Presidents of public companies, relying on investment, regularly meet major investors, who insist they hear from the senior manager. Although donors don't want information overload, they really want to speak with the leader.

8. You learn through the process.

Leaders can be storytellers. In telling the story, you shape and refine your message: you get better at it. Every time you meet a person and give your story, you learn what is missing, not in the story but in the plans on which the story is based.

◆ ◆ ◆

I sat with the president of a major Canadian family business, a man who was outside of our Christian tradition. I opened with, "I think what we are doing will be of interest to you. We are doing something that hasn't been done in Toronto in over a hundred years."

From my reading of the Jesuits' story of building educational communities, I understood that training builds long-lasting Christian values into young people. But it wasn't just any form of education; it had a deliberate set of ingredients that shape the way people think, live, and serve. At Tyndale, we agreed that in building the college into a university three elements were indispensable: sharpening the mind, cultivating the character, and nurturing the heart of faith.

The concept crystallized when an early investor gave me a copy of Heroic Leadership *by Chris Lowney. The idea became a door opener and helped me formulate to others what we had in mind. As I spoke to this donor, the description resonated as he understood it was an educational offering young people would not get in most other places in this city: an education that respects the spiritual along with intellect and character. The idea was generic to our historic view of education, but it was this early investor who helped me in the making of this formulation.*

◆ ◆ ◆

9. It develops networks.

Developing networks provides a leader with connections that help in many ways. Contacts will build relationships, some of which will last for life. Don't assume the role of a spiritual counselor, but be responsive when people turn to you for confidential counsel. I benefit from friends who speak wisdom, faith, and encouragement into my life. I gain much more from these relationships than I give.

10. It develops other kinds of support.

Though I have spoken of money in resource development, recruiting people as volunteers and for prayer support happens in the same way as donor development. When leaders are rooted in and open about expressing faith, meeting with donors will cultivate prayerful partners—not surprising, because where people put their treasure, that is where their hearts will be.

WHAT IS RESOURCE DEVELOPMENT?

ARTICULATING YOUR MISSION

You may know what you want to accomplish, but until you define it in brief, compelling terms it will be wind and fury. An idea may lift your spirits and drive your energy, but until tested and retested, it may be a bundle of nerves wrapped up in conversation. A simple test is the *elevator speech*. Can you describe the mission within a ten-floor elevator ride? If not, the statement may be too abstract.

LIVING THE LIFE

Giving isn't a result of a smooth presentation; it comes from people attracted to a cause. The talk and walk of your organization must match. By investing in your enterprise, a donor takes a risk. Ponzi schemes are reminders that we all live on the raw edge of trust. What evidence do you give to donors that you are reliable? Ask those who support your mission: What first attracted them to invest? What sustains their giving? What more would they need to be assured that their trust is well placed?

LIFTING PEOPLE'S EYES TO THE LARGER ISSUE

Leaders invite people to the walk of faith. Sometimes the response is "go away money"—that is, a very modest amount just to get rid of you.

Human impulse is to give when it is convenient and what is comfortable. To discomfort people in their giving is not to exert pressure; rather it is to enlarge their understanding of what together you are capable of doing.

LIVING THE PART AS A SHEPHERD AND SERVANT

Leaders fulfill two important roles: shepherd and servant.

A shepherd, even though regarded as shady and untrustworthy in Jesus' time, still symbolized care for the flock: the flock supplied the shepherd with income and in turn was cared for.

A servant (in a time when there was no middle class) was less like a waiter and more like an indentured slave. To be called to be a servant was not a pleasant reference for those who listened to Jesus. His point was that leaders were not to be like the imposed outsiders from Rome or the politically appointed high priests or the few who had (often misappropriated) wealth and amassed property. They were to be those who did menial work.

These two powerful metaphors help us consider who we are to be.

TELLING THE STORY

Raising funds is a by-product of storytelling. People give to what makes a difference. My generation had loyalty to institutions. The following generation moved from institutional giving to cause giving, looking for ways in which an investment would have impact.

As chief storyteller, tell

◆ of the past: people like to know the essence of an organization's journey—the people and critical movements it was involved with.

◆ of the present: you'll be amazed at how people are interested in knowing what is going on now; notice how people cluster around a camera to see a picture taken fifteen seconds earlier.

◆ of the future: describe what the organization or project will look like in five or ten years.

After the story is adequately told, make "the ask," keeping this simple rule in mind: once the request has been made, be quiet. Resist the impulse to fill the silence. Allow the donor to comment first. You have done your best to put the case. Now sit back and let the donor decide what to do or say. Pressure is unacceptable. Your work, for the time, is done. If the response is uncertain, there may be opportunity for more information or time for further consideration.

They are the donor's resources, after all. You have no right to them. The gift that will or will not be made is for that person to decide. In your enthusiasm and eagerness, don't ruin future opportunities or friendship by trying to push for a decision.

A WORD TO PASTORS

Don't avoid the subject of giving. Your church tradition may have developed its own pattern of talking about money. Note how often Jesus discussed money. This is not a rationale to pressure your people into giving to your annual fund or a campaign. As pastors, you enrich your members by providing biblical counsel on finances. Tell me a person's giving patterns and I can tell you something about the person's spiritual life. Some people will give to exert influence. Don't let that keep you from seeing teaching on money as critical to your instruction on Christian discipleship.

The biblical phrase "The storehouse of the Lord" is not synonymous with the local congregation. As much as church attendees should give generously to the work of their own congregation, giving isn't about that alone. As you raise the matter of giving beyond your local activities, and lift it into the wider world, people will be less defensive, knowing that your teaching on giving is not for your enterprise but offered so that they will be enabled to live a more healthy Christian life.

A WORD TO CEOs AND BOARDS OF CHARITIES

Avoid the mistake of thinking that people owe you support. Among organizations specializing in caring for the poor, sick, and needy, and those focused on justice and mercy, there is an often subtle assumption that because good is being done, people *should* stand alongside in their support.

Resources become available when they are recruited. The biblical text makes that clear: *we lack because we don't ask*. Balance trust in God with actual fund-raising. I've made my case on trusting God. Such trust is essential to leadership. But some leaders use religious language to put forward a case that they need not work at fund-raising but only "trust" for the resources to come in. That attitude, however, is like a farmer who simply declares trust in God for the harvest, with no need to work the land, plant the seed, control the weeds, or ensure adequate moisture.

◆ ◆ ◆

Once Tyndale had agreed to purchase the campus from the Sisters of St Joseph, we knew we needed to raise more than the purchase price. We decided on a goal of $58 million. I choked. Here we were, a small university/seminary less that a decade out of bankruptcy. In a previous year, we had a small campaign of $12 million, raised mainly by Ruth Whitt and I setting appointments and making requests. This new goal pushed us into a new zone.

We knew we had no choice but to proceed. But on what basis? What would be the underlying assumptions?

This was a deeply spiritual decision and process. We knew we didn't have sufficient contacts. As well, as president, I knew that the major weight of making calls and requests was mine to lift. The Old Testament story of Joshua, the one I noted earlier, became my touchstone of faith. As God instructed the Israelite leader Joshua to get them across the Jordan River into the Promised Land, his promise was, "When the priests step into the water, then I will stop the river." This story had been the spark to my coming to Tyndale, and it continued to be a source of illumination for decisions and choices.

Again and again, we returned to the story. The campaign was an act of faith. If we failed, we could imagine the enormous embarrassment it would bring to the witness of Christ and the community we served.

We carefully worked our way through important stages of the journey.

First we got the message right. As spectacular as was the new campus, as stunning as was the chapel, philanthropists look at their gifts with a tough eye to value and purpose. It took us months to wrestle with the message of the campaign.

Then we established a group who let us use their names and were willing to refer us to possible donors and make a few calls themselves. This helped to position us in communities beyond our usual connections.

We knew that to get the campaign rolling we needed a few major investments. As much as the smaller gifts mattered, for this campaign we needed larger gifts to begin to move forward. A few families, understanding the historic nature of this opportunity, and believing in the training of young people for life and ministry, pledged gifts that quickly moved us into the twenty-million-dollar range. This demonstrated to others that people respected for their business acumen believed in the institution and were willing to invest major gifts. This brought an acceleration of meetings and gifts.

I learned that unless people viewed this project in terms larger than they had ever planned, we simply would not make the target. In meeting after meeting, telling the story from the start, how Lily had first seen this campus with an eye of faith and then the board had caught the vision, I asked donors to look beyond the total amount and give in light of the goal.

In time, the message was refined and I better understood what mattered in the telling. This became key as we met with those who knew little of our history and less of our ethos. Telling the story invited them into what Tyndale had been and encouraged them to project themselves into its life and future.

PRINCIPLE 7

Recognize the Politics

I've learned in leading not-for-profit organizations that, while politics isn't everything, everything is political.

Nehemiah lived in a world of political intrigue, so when the darts and arrows of political opposition came his way he wasn't surprised. Sanballat, head of Samaria, along with co-conspirator Tobiah, ridiculed the Jews for talk of rebuilding the city walls. Ridicule Nehemiah could take. However, when the opposition became hostile, he divided the workers, half building the wall and the other half standing watch.

It was internal politics that was a major strain for Nehemiah: Jews exploiting each other with unfair usury, forcing families to sell children for food or mortgage their fields, vineyards, and homes just to survive the famine. Rebuilding the wall meant that Jewish communities, often estranged in the past, now had to work and live together. That led to disagreement. Politics, he understood, was not something to avoid but embrace.

WHAT IS POLITICS?

Politics is the interface of people as they live together. Sometimes it's harmonious, other times difficult and even nasty. While ideas are magnets around which people can coalesce as a community or a team, people make the ideas work, and it is here that the internal dynamics of political interface come into play.

Language about politics was crafted by the Greeks. Aristotle used the word *politika,* later Romanized into the Latin *politicus,* from which we get the idea of citizens (*polites*) living within a city (*polis*) or a governed community.

To set it in perspective and understand politics as an essential ingredient of community life, let's understand it to mean *the human dynamics at play as people work together in pursuit of common objectives.*

Politics is at work when leaders do their job of setting goals, establishing boundaries, negotiating terms and agreements, harmonizing activities, ensuring order, protecting the community, establishing discipline, creating means of celebration and rewards, to name a few of the leadership tasks.

If there is a disagreement between senior staff and the leader, and the staff meet together to discuss their concerns, that is political, a natural way to find a solution. Sometimes people do this with sensitivity and care, and other times not. Toward the end of my time with Youth for Christ, senior staff were frustrated with my leadership. They met and assigned the responsibility to speak with me to one person. My reaction was, "They're playing politics," because I didn't appreciate what they had to say. But what was their option? They were not "playing" politics in that they were manipulating matters for their own benefit. They were exercising their rightful political presence, seeking a solution.

Politics as a discipline and exercise is the means by which the body politic, the group, lives and finds ways to do what is needed to accomplish agreed-on goals. It is not finding the lowest common denominator—although that may be needed as a start in order to bring people together. It is about people getting along, finding appropriate ways of working together.

POLITICS IS EVERYWHERE

By the very nature of living in family and society (local, national, and international) ours is a political world. When people enter a group, they bring their experiences, biases, hopes, and means of acting.

I was asked to chair a parents' meeting held by a church board that had announced in December that the school, which was part of the church organization, would no longer be able to hold classes in the church building the following September. There was enormous upset, so the board agreed to hold an information meeting. About 800 people, mostly parents, showed up. For five hours they asked questions and expressed their concerns.

There were enormous misunderstandings at all levels. Parents were upset, many acting in anger, assuming the administration's actions were malicious. Rumors abounded. Accusations were slung. Motives were questioned. Feelings ran high.

Was it a good meeting? It will depends on whom you ask. But it was politics at work. The community had an issue that needed public airing.

Community is about living and working together, and the interaction of people requires rules, conversation, accountability, and honest exchange of ideas. In most groups there will be a variety of views on most issues, and these will range along the whole spectrum. Theologically conservative communities are often conservative in political, economic, and social views as well. The parallel is true for those of a more liberal theology. Yet it's a mistake to assume that one label fits all. Leaders allow people their variegated views without assuming or insisting they correspond with the leaders' own views.

Leaders make sense of problems, organize personnel, oversee the project, and manage its collateral aspects. Know as well that eventually you will be a target. Though I had not been around when Tyndale collapsed and had had no part in creating its governance difficulties, I was the one people could turn to. Rumor mills ground on. Backroom conversations crafted scenarios and possibilities that I had to decipher, respond to, or ignore. Politics was very much at work.

It wasn't because it was the worst of times, for even in the best of times, political dynamics is a factor of human community. Accept it. Define it. Encourage it. Guide it. And learn to enjoy the interplay as you lead.

LEADING IN A POLITICAL ENVIRONMENT

People need structure, authority, defined assignment, accountability, and empowerment. In a wide range of organizational types—from Machiavelli's absolute power to flat-line egalitarianism—each of us is somewhere in between. We each choose our model depending on various factors: history, ethnicity, religious experiences, location of operation, required guidelines of operation, and sophistication of our society, among others. Regardless of the model, political reality runs through it and, if used wisely, will provide leverage for effective leadership. Your success in part will depend on developing a structure that includes and sufficiently amplifies authority, defined assignment, accountability, and empowerment.

So how do you go about leading, knowing that all things are political?

Begin with a point of reference to which the whole life and activity of the enterprise refer. Don't assume that what you had thirty-six months ago is in play today. Organizations are not static. The strategy needs reviewing each year and the mission statement at least every five years.

In a previous chapter I outlined the GOST approach to planning: goals, objectives, strategies, and tactics. In considering political dynamics, in this chapter I'm shifting to a model that begins with *vision*. Experience tells me that when I wrestle with political interactions that could lead to disaster, one (or more) of the defining aspects of the project or organization—vision, values, mission, goals—is either unclear or non-existent.

As a concrete example to assist us in thinking about holding the political dynamic in check, I use the managing of a space agency.

VISION

Vision defines the organization. When the vision is clear and agreed on, it calls on everyone to check whether what is being done is in line with the vision.

President Kennedy said the mission of the U.S. space program was to go to the moon. However, that wasn't the mission; nor was it the vision. It was the goal. The vision and mission gave logical rise to the idea of going to the moon, which as a goal was a subset of the vision.

The vision might have read "To explore space for the betterment of humankind."

A vision is not enterprise exclusive. Other organizations may have one similar to yours. At Tyndale, our first vision statement was "To educate and equip Christians to serve the world with passion for Jesus Christ." From time to time, I would exegete it, word by word, for students, staff, faculty, and donors. Ten years later, after becoming a university, we broadened it to the following, to better define who we had become.

Tyndale is dedicated

> to the pursuit of truth,

> to excellence in teaching, learning and research, for the enriching of mind, heart and character,

to serve the church and the world

for the glory of God.

Vision is what we are about.

VALUES

Values are the things that matter to us and enable the organization to check up on whether the way something is being done corresponds to the organization's values.

In running an international space agency, we might include the following as the values:

- respect for the environment

- care for human life

- honesty in describing to the public what we discover

- careful use of resources

- honesty as a broker among nations

- courage to go beyond safe borders

The reason values matter to political well-being is that, while vision may be understood, the organization needs agreement as to what it holds dear. Values are the glue, solidifying the elements that members of the group agree matter.

MISSION

Mission translates vision into the tangible. Most people don't live in the high atmosphere of vision. They need something more specific but broad enough to allow initiative, imagination, and creativity.

Continuing with the space agency as our example, mission might include

- learning whether there are other forms of life in the universe

- understanding the development of structures involved in planet formation

- building sustainable human life zones in outer space

- inventing means of travel outside of carbon-based fuels

Politically, defining mission matters. As harmony exists with vision and values, identifying mission helps clear away clutter that can provoke political infighting.

GOALS

Goals define what we seek to accomplish, the timeline, and specifics that match up departments, people, resources. It is goals that we measure in short-term evaluations.

Our space agency goals might include the following:

- Within five years build a self-supporting community on the moon.

- Within ten years invent self-directing and self-sustaining cameras that can travel for a hundred years and regularly send pictures to Earth.

- Within fifteen years land a person on Mars.

Advancing into the details of goals and the attached timelines and person(s) responsible moves people forward. Indecision promotes speculation. Speculation and the lack of diligence are a sure environment for political dysfunction.

STRATEGIC MOVES FOR POLITICAL LEADERSHIP

Leaders, particularly those who are rebuilding, inevitably run into resistance: people tired, upset, and discouraged dig in their heels, acting in negative and unappreciative ways.

Ron Heifetz and Marty Linsky, in *Leadership on the Line*, suggest strategic moves to help make political factors an advantage. I've incorporated some of their ideas along with some insights of my own.

Know that for some, new ideas will be unnerving. People in the throes of failure, anxious about their immediate finances and long-term security, may be frightened of your new and bold ideas. Teach them about risk, what it means to live by faith. In so doing you will teach them how to live in the present calamity and for life.

Work to overcome the status quo. After the fall of the Berlin Wall and demise of the Soviet empire, many eastern Europeans said they preferred order to freedom, old ways to disorder, and certainty of what they had to uncertainty of the new. The present, with its knowns and predictability, is the chosen default for some. Their resistance to moving out of today's world into a time and place they can't see necessitates hand-holding. As leader, show them the advantages of rebuilding and how you will get there.

Help people articulate their views and needs. In my early days at Tyndale I sensed the anger at past leadership that had allowed it to tip into receivership. After hearing staff grievances, I realized that some of them knew much about how an operation should work, and we needed their wisdom and expertise.

When dealing with a broken or discouraged organization, its members, staff, and volunteers need your empathy. Assure them you understand their personal loss and avoid conversation on who was responsible. Remind them no one intentionally set out to fail.

Create a safe place where people can offer opinions without fear of jeopardizing their positions. Construct the work environment so everyone knows how it works, providing freedom for expression so people will be heard, all the while reminding them they are responsible for what they say.

Meet with the community at agreed-on times. Create an expectation that at certain times of the year there will be town hall meetings. Keep that time sacred for you and your people, and agree on the rules of engagement so there are no surprises.

Control the temperature. High temperature is not always bad. However, if a heated environment becomes the norm, it may skew the conversation and disrupt your ability to guide the process.

How can you control the temperature? As you plan a meeting, whether with a department, with heads of departments, or a town hall meeting, agree at the start on what is allowed, defining rules that will frame the conversation.

Pace the work. In times of stress, people may react in ways not in tune with their life patterns and say what they would never say in less-pressured times. Each of us has personal tolerance levels in accepting change and the speed of change.

Trying too hard to reach your goal in the allotted time frame may be counterproductive, and timelines may need to be revised. Slow down if the pace is creating too much unsettledness. Gauge the drive to move forward by the political ease or tension it creates.

Anticipate fallout. Organizational or business trauma inevitably results in the loss of good people, sometimes your best. As much as you will try to find a suitable role for everyone, some won't be able to ride the rough journey into the future. If they can't dislodge the negative baggage of the past, it is probably best that they leave. Give them your blessing and get on with finding those you need.

Identify the disparate groups within the organization. If you have come up through the organization, you've experienced the group dynamics peculiar to the organization and you recognize where polarizations are likely to occur when interests are at variance.

To better understand the various groups, list who they are within the organization. Some will be obvious, defined by a department or affinity. Others will be hidden in the organizational woodwork as smaller entities, unnoticed within the larger groupings.

Once you've discerned who the groups are, do some testing. Ask what they would plan if they were in charge.

Note how groups operate. The business office will have a different modus operandi from sales or marketing. Their responsibilities will give rise to strategies different from other departments. They will recruit different personalities. Take time to learn what makes a good member of a financial team in contrast to one from marketing, for example. Then watch how they interact with each other.

Develop an agreement with the governing board, defining its role in governance and yours in management. There are various theories on the relationship of governance to management, some egalitarian, others more hierarchical. In addition, each leader operates with a personality that calls for tailoring the agreement on lines of authority and expectations of the board. You might be inclined to suppose that your previous experience will work in your new situation, that the people you're working with now will be like those you worked with in the past and that they understand what you want or expect. Don't assume. Clarify regularly and test out the workings of the agreement. Without that, the relationship can develop into the worst of political nightmares.

Identify spiritual opposition. Don't dismiss evil as nothing but a metaphor. Sophisticated societies framed by a material world assume the nonmaterial world is spooky, unknowable, a figment of overactive minds. For 2,000 years the Christian community has developed a body of knowledge and disciplines of practice in identifying how to be protected and empowered by the Spirit.

Learn from jazz. Leadership is both science and art, but mostly art. The science of leading involves learning which levers help you exercise authority, power, and influence. Leaders operating on intuition driven by enthusiasm can inadvertently be blind to learning the discipline of leadership. If you are egregiously self-confident, assuming that learning this science is unnecessary, you may lose a valuable ingredient in the mix of your leadership.

Leadership is also improvisational. In our Saskatoon church I couldn't get enough of music. Along with my two brothers and two sisters, I took piano lessons. I studied classical and gospel, but jazz became my love.

Jazz is extraordinary. To some it sounds complex, without melody or harmony. Actually it is an outflow of classical music, especially the contrapuntal form crafted by John Sebastian Bach, which takes a theme, or melody line, and works it through the composition. Listen to a Bach fugue or invention and you will hear the melody line moving back and forth. It then takes on added musical features, but all the while the melody remains.

Jazz adds improvisation. The melody moves its way through interpretations of the trio or quartet. Listen to the late pianist Oscar Peterson: he plays the melody line, and then it moves on to others in the combo, one by one. They layer the tune with additional material, with improvisation.

It isn't a novice who can improvise. Peterson could because he knew the science as well as the art. His discipline, experience, and creative talent allowed him to improvise.

So it is with leadership. We improvise. Effective leaders understand that it isn't about them. It's about internal interplay of ideas, personalities, needs, and possibilities. We listen, watch, and then, when appropriate, move ideas around, start or stop conversation, turn to someone who is listening without adding much, and ask for input. Know when to push and when to pull. Feel when it is time to be tough and disciplined or when to relax and party. Trust your instincts. Be flexible on time and performance. You have the right and responsibility to improvise. It will enhance your ability to move politically among ideas, personalities, and issues outside your control.

DEALING WITH THE DYNAMICS OF THE BODY POLITIC

How does leadership handle political dynamics?

Seek out those with whom you can dependably collaborate. During my first week at Tyndale I met Nita Stemmler, who worked in the bookstore. I learned that she not only had a deep love for the schools but also had a grasp of the issues (many of them political) needing my attention. I asked her to put together a list of issues we needed to address. For months I carried it with me. Periodically we would go over it, measuring our progress.

Ask for ideas on a plan to move forward. Drill down into the experience, passion, and talent of people on staff, both paid and volunteer.

Keep close to those you know oppose you. People who seem to be on the opposite side may not be enemies. They may have important solutions. If you regard them as enemies, the broken relationships may fester and lead to more disruption. Give the "opponents" a chance. Ask them what they would do in your position.

Stay in communication, reminding people of the past, present, and future stories. Telling stories helps people know where they stand within the body politic. Frame for people who you all are, where you are going, and where they fit into the scheme. History matters. Learn the past, what made the organization good and effective. Draw on that memory. Then describe where you are. Be kind but blunt. Don't gloss over the facts, but don't leave them there. Etch out an outline of what the future may very well be. As disgruntled as some may be, you can rightfully assume that people want to be part of a winning and successful enterprise. Speak hope. Take your people to a level where they can see the landscape and its possibilities.

Anticipate that personalities will clash. "Dirty" politics usually happen as people come to dislike each other. Work into your schedule times for open conversation and for partying. Allow people to air their concerns in a way that is not threatening to them and their future, yet responsible enough that it doesn't become a grouching session. Then find excuses to celebrate.

Allow conflict to work its way through to resolution. Human dynamics are complex, interlocked with all kinds of emotions, memories, competitive personalities, and egos. If your reaction is to fix them today, rein that in. Some things take care of themselves.

Sometimes take the way of least resistance. Mentor and friend Bob Cooley identified this as important in conflict. At first I resisted the idea. Then, realizing its counterintuitive value, I found that at times it is best to do nothing and allow the workings of human interrelationships to operate. But know when it is time to step in. Choose when to resist. Wait for a time when it is worth spending political capital.

Take your stakeholders up to a higher point of view. Most of us live so close to the ground we lose sight of the wider landscape; this is especially true for managers. Lift them above circumstances, problems, and conflicts and—again by story—help them see what life looks like from there. Politics can be influenced by feeding into conversations information on what the point of contention looks like to others and how it can be interpreted from a broader point of view.

Don't take things personally. If you are "thin-skinned," prone to letting people's comments rule your spirit, ask someone to help make sense of what you are hearing and how you are reacting. If negative comments become habitual chattering voices, and if you give them space in your hearing, the voice of your calling may be drowned by their noise.

Refuse to allow special deals in your attempt to keep someone onside. Negotiation helps the body politic function. Even so, I once got into danger by crafting a deal that helped to assuage one person but resulted in misunderstanding within the group. I have no guidelines on this; I simply advise caution and discernment.

Respect and affirm the board and its role. Leaders can get unduly focused on their own responsibilities and forget that ultimate authority is vested in the board of governors, trustees, or elders.

Don't allow situations to create a rift between you and the governance body. In times when there is misunderstanding or conflict between leader and board, the leader may be tempted to represent the board to staff in such a way as to get the staff on his or her "side," and in so doing create friction that can lead to irresolvable difficulty. Disagreements with the board are to be worked out behind closed doors. Always affirm the board's authority.

You will want political stability within the authority framework. Your relationship with the governance group is as important as any, and working with them is as strategic as anything you do. To ensure that the proper governance–administration structure is in place, allow time and thought for your working relationship with the board; work to strengthen its membership and increase their knowledge of the enterprise, thus cementing an effective partnership.

Politics are particularly in play in the dynamics linking you to governance. As leader (or CEO) you are the primary link between administration and the governing body. Authority and responsibility flow both ways. From the governors (board) you receive authority and responsibility to oversee the operation. It works the other way as well. The operation (staff) gives you authority and responsibility (power) by their willingness to serve under your leadership. If they reject your leadership, you lose your authority to lead. You need their cooperation and support. As the board sees your leadership affirmed, they have more reason to trust you. Staff empower you. It is a relationship in which politics is vital.

Keep the board from interfering with management. There is a fine line that separates governance and management. Don't assume that either side knows where that line is. Raise it regularly with your chair and board, discussing respective roles of board and management, how each side is reading the other, and the comfort level with how the two sides interface.

Admit your mistakes. Others see our errors, misjudgments, lack of insight, and occasional misspoken ideas, so we might as well admit them. Don't wallow in errors, but be up front with your senior staff and, when appropriate, let your board know. Invite them to identify areas of vulnerability; then agree on a regular time in which you answer their concerns in light of progress. Strike a balance. A little self-deprecating humor can go a long way.

Identify your assumptions. Political leadership (and remember, all leadership is political) works best when your team agrees on your working assumptions: vision, values, mission, and goals. If I were to walk into your enterprise and ask you what they are, could you produce a written copy? And more, if I asked a staff member what they are, would he or she know they exist, be able to identify one or two, or know where to find a copy?

CONDITIONS FOR EFFECTIVE LEADERSHIP

Who is in charge? Leaders lead—at least this is what we expect. However, when the elements required to lead effectively are not defined or understood, political instability results.

Ask your group if there is clarity on authority, defined assignment, accountability, and empowerment. These four pillars of an enterprise provide you as leader with a base on which political interaction will benefit your leadership and work.

Authority is the right granted to a person to do what is asked. It comes from others either in a formal sense—a job description and a board or congregation—or informally when people assess your ability to lead and agree to fall in line with where you are going.

Established authority helps to clear the air when people question who is ultimately in charge. Political instability occurs when the leader has written authority but not informal authority.

Defined assignment is management making it clear for staff what is expected, ensuring that employees understand assignments. While this seems self-evident, people and organizations fall into abusive and discordant relationships when people don't know what is expected. Defining an assignment is more than a written job description. It requires revisiting the commitment regularly so that leader and staff both know what is expected. Nasty political testiness can be averted when people know what they and others are doing.

Accountability is both attitude and process: attitude in that people expect and accept that they and others will be held accountable, and process in carrying out preset reviews. It has been found, both in for profit and nonprofit organizations, that salary and benefits are not the determining factor in staff retention. Critical to retention is people being held accountable. It is like compensation, in effect saying, "You matter enough for me to make the effort to evaluate how and what you are doing." Employees learn they are valued.

Empowerment links assignment with adequate social, technical, and emotional tools. If you ask someone to dig a trench but don't supply a shovel, at the end of the day you both will be frustrated and disappointed. Empowering staff sets them free to meet goals.

YOUR LEADERSHIP TEAM: KEY TO POLITICAL MANAGEMENT

In the mid 1980s, Leighton Ford, chair of the Lausanne Committee for World Evangelization, asked me to organize a world event to find and encourage 350 younger and emerging leaders in the Christian community, to be held in Singapore in May 1987. I assembled a worldwide 18-member planning team, meeting for a couple of years. In our 1985 meeting in Stuttgart, Germany, after two days of conflict and disagreement, I said, "I'm going to have to tell Leighton that this won't work; it seems this will never get off the ground."

Conversation ground to a halt. The fiery words and self-possessed speeches ended. Elie Lau from Hong Kong spoke up. In a few minutes of impassioned pleading, she implored each member to lay down personal agendas and, as members of a single team, make it work. I never did speak with Leighton about what seemed sure disaster. The team decided that what we were about was too important to allow the stress and strain of international differences torpedo the project.

Positive political dynamics within a team rest on a number of measures.

◆ Build a sense of community, of belonging. A tribal instinct allows people to retain identity and a sense of being while operating together in a team-like way.

◆ Allow team members to feel their freedom to operate without a sense of being dominated and overtaken by the leader. This will ease the inclination for political infighting.

◆ Avoid sabotaging ideas and initiatives. The team is not there to serve your self-interests or massage your ego. Inevitably there will be competition for your approval and support. Alienating team members by dismissing ideas only fractures relationships.

- If something goes wrong, don't hide behind the team's decisions. The team will see you as politically weak, unable to stand up to your failures or indecisions.

- Listen, then contribute, recognizing there is a balance between hearing the views of others and spouting your own. Consciously listen and let the team know you are listening. A response like "Let me repeat what you said to make sure I understood it clearly" is a helpful way to send a message that indeed you are listening. The political value is that it breeds inclusion of ideas and ownership.

- Make the team essential to your plan. The team you create reflects you. Identification with the team is not to be done after success is assured; it happens in process.

- Understand systemic rules that govern group behavior. The dynamics of a group are different from those when individuals operate on their own. In addition, groups vary from one to another.

Recognize that guiding a team is something different from running an organization. While the team is part of the organization, it is family, working with lines of authority and responsibility that run alongside each other.

- As much as you may want to be one of them, and in a sense you are, in another sense you aren't "one of the girls—or boys." You are a senior among equals.

- Know that, for most, being part of a team is one of the most deeply satisfying parts of an assignment.

- Help team members know that because they are part of a team, they aren't on their own. Accomplishments are shared.

- Be aware that teams will struggle in making it work. Building a team is not for perfection. It is to accomplish a task.

- As you build and manage the team, provide times for built-up steam to be let off.

- Have the team evaluate its own work and progress.

- Work at making meetings something to look forward to, interspersed with ideas, prayer, readings, food, and celebration where participants feel privileged to be members.

◆ ◆ ◆

In building Tyndale University, our cabinet and board agreed that creating a degree in education was strategic to our reputation and programs. It fit with our vision and the importance of developing a university that trained graduates to go into the wider society as Christians.

So we began. We invested over a half million dollars in research and development. Led by provost Earl Davey and organized by my sister Joni Patterson, a retired school principal, the team put together what we hoped would be among the finest bachelor of education degrees offered in Ontario.

The political structure in Canada puts responsibility for education in the hands of the province. We passed the first hurdle, approved by the Postsecondary Education Quality Assessment Board. The next step was for the minister of training, colleges, and universities to write a letter to the Ontario College of Teachers to do their due diligence on our application and, if approved, accredit us for offering the degree in education.

As we waited and waited, we realized something was wrong. Despite our attempts to connect with the minister and his department, we got no comment. We needed to know if there was a problem, and if there was, what we could do to fix it. The clock was ticking. We had invested a huge amount of money (by anyone's standards) and needed to set in motion recruitment of students and faculty.

Stuck, we hired a consulting firm to uncover the problem. Months later we learned there were two issues: one was policy and the second was that the minister showed no interest in getting to our file.

On the policy matter, our chancellor, the Honorable Jake Epp, got me an appointment with the senior policy advisor to the premier. Within fifteen minutes, over a coffee in a Starbucks, we solved the policy matter. The bigger political problem was getting a fair and honest response from the minister.

Time dragged on. Finally, working with our local member of provincial parliament (MPP), we learned that the minister had no intention of forwarding our application to the College of Teachers. Without their accreditation our plans were dead.

So what could we do? We didn't know whether the minister was being unfair to us because we were Christian or if there was another reason for his refusal to process our application or even speak to us or allow one of his people to let us know the reason for his decision.

I spoke to our cabinet and board and said I believed we needed to exercise political wisdom and force to get the rationale for the government's (specifically, the minister's) decision. There was concern that such steps might not be appropriate Christian spirit and form. I agreed. But I also believed that an injustice was being done.

As it happened, it was a year before the next provincial election, and the party in power was concerned with what they called "the ethnic vote," by which they specifically meant the Chinese, Korean, and Black communities. In Toronto, several large churches of these communities were pastored by our graduates.

I invited a few pastors together, told them of our problem, and asked if they would help. They were enthusiastic to do so. First we met with our MPP. He was more than willing to help and to take this to a senior minister, especially as he saw the numbers of voters these churches represented. We came to understand that to exert political influence on the minister responsible for education, we had to convince his cabinet colleagues and the premier. So we met with other senior cabinet ministers, putting forth our case, all the while hearing nothing from the minister concerned.

As the weeks dragged on, I came to learn that a young Christian assistant to our MPP was working behind the scenes, pressing the assistant to the finance minister (and chair of the coming election campaign) for a meeting. In time it came.

A dozen pastors and I had gathered around finance minister Greg Sorbara's board table at Queen's Park, the legislative buildings. I outlined the problem. The minister went around the table, asking each pastor some questions, essentially learning the size of their church communities. Then quietly, without any prompting, a pastor spoke up and said, "Minister, Tyndale matters to us very much, and if we feel you are being unfair to them, we will remember you next fall."

It came so unexpectedly, clear and unrehearsed. The minister smiled and asked, "Brian, what is your timeline?"

151

Some weeks later, after the minister of training, colleges and universities had changed his mind and given us permission, I spoke with a member of his political team and asked if we had any friends left at the minister's office. "Oh yes," came the reply. "We see you as a player."

"And what is a player?" I asked.

"One who can turn the minister 180 degrees without embarrassing him publicly."

As part of the body politic of this province, and knowing that our way forward was being blocked (for what reason we never did learn), we believed it was appropriate and within the mandate of our university and fair as a follower of Jesus to press the point in a polite and gracious way, ever asking that we be treated fairly and justly.

While politics isn't everything, everything is political.

CHAPTER 8

Evaluate Your Achievement

CONSIDERING SUCCESS

Achieving success is not a single exercise, for measurements are both internal—what one experiences in doing—and external—the views of others.

I reflected on that while driving home from a farewell dinner given by the board of Tyndale. The evening, as one might expect, was devoted to what had transpired over the previous fourteen years. We had written a new and vigorous mission statement. The reputation of Tyndale had grown. We were proud of our graduates, serving worldwide. The college had been transformed into a university, and the seminary had grown. A new campus had been purchased, and the institution was well on its way to completion of the capital campaign. We had moved from bankruptcy to fourteen years of continuous balanced budgets. There was no debt. The balance sheet looked good. Nice words were said. I looked over the past with memories of happiness and disappointments, accepting that these years had been successful, judging from both the internal and external.

In that moment I asked, Can it be said these years were successful? Successful for whom? Surely it wasn't my success, because many had contributed, even those who were leading when the schools got into trouble. They had kept it going. I arrived at a time and in an opportune moment when it was positioned to go to the next stage. The financial collapse was a gift. In receivership we could initiate what couldn't have been done otherwise. Those who were part of the past were part of its eventual success and deserved credit.

However, the full picture wasn't painted at the farewell dinner. Retirement dinners never do tell the whole story. The real story includes failures, inadequacies, imperfections, as those close to me could testify.

How does one measure one's leadership?

Nehemiah's life is a template of ideas, motivations, and principles that provide opportunity for reflection.

In taking an ancient story and creating a paradigm of action, one must be wary of reading into the story, fabricating an outline that goes beyond what the writer wanted to say in the first place. Whether I have crossed that borderline of fabrication, I leave for you to decide.

In these final pages, linking Nehemiah of ancient Persia with decades of my own leadership, mostly in Canada, I conclude with what I consider to be valuable in leadership.

MEASURING SUCCESS

For those embarking on leadership, for those currently leading, and for those closer to the end, I offer these six tests.

HAVE I BEEN FAITHFUL TO MY CALL?

At Tyndale the call was external: the board of governors invited me to the position. It was also internal: Lily and I agreed in a conversation while driving in Florida on a March afternoon in 1996.

Overarching those specifics is the lifelong call of the Spirit to public ministry and service. The call to Tyndale didn't begin the day Geoff Moore and I had our conversation at the Billy Graham reception. It began much earlier. As a child, I knew my life would be spent in church-related ministry, a call refined over time and in ways I never imagined.

Have I been faithful to this call for lifetime service? One's lack of discernment, due to intellectual incapacity, insecurities, pride, selfishness, to name a few, break up the road of service like oversized gravel, chipping the paint, wearing the tires, and from time to time disabling the car.

Our frail human condition will at times short-circuit our call; yet we start again and find, in following our master, a renewed desire.

Thomas Harris's book *I'm OK, You're OK* soared on a 1970s societal craze for feeling good. Self-fulfillment became a litmus test for success. Christians shaped by this *zeitgeist* interpret God's call based on self-fulfillment. Nothing so belies the biblical call and turns spiritual well-being inside out as assuming that if we feel fulfilled we must be within God's will. Or conversely, if we don't, we've missed it by a mile.

Friends wanting to know the state of my being would ask, "Are you enjoying your work?" At times I responded with, "Please ask, 'Are you doing what you should be doing?'"

There are periods in which we feel rewarded, experience the blush of success, sense that our work is in concert with God's grand scheme. But that's not our best gauge. Such times come momentarily and are gone. Some experiences produce self-doubt. Many decisions come by agonizing reflection. There are decisions that committees, let alone manuals, don't solve. Leaders are called on—often alone—to deal with those.

Self-fulfillment may be a by-product of leading. But if you make it the test of being in God's will, you will be tempted to "hear" God's call to "sunnier" climates, to places far from troubled front lines, to people who like you and make you feel important.

I can't read the eleventh chapter of Hebrews and then live with a sense of entitlement that self-fulfillment is my right as God's servant. "These were all commended for their faith, yet none of them received what had been promised."

What is success then? For that measurement I look to the external, to those to whom I'm accountable. Write a means of periodic evaluation into the agenda of your board. Keep up to speed with how they rate your leadership.

Success is also measured by the community you serve. Inevitably we hear from them, good or bad. Given that my work took me into churches, pastors' conferences, and meeting with agencies and denominations, I heard words of encouragement, advice, counsel, and occasionally rebuke.

Internal measurement is so varied, given our personal feelings, that it makes it difficult to run any sort of measuring tape there. Yet, to sense within yourself that you are or have been successful, as viewed against your objectives, is important. Keeping a journal will give you, over time, a sense of how you see the success of your life and work.

So to answer the question, yes, after almost five decades of service in various ministries I have been faithful to the Call. Faithfulness in large part defined by desire and drive while candidly admitting that failures and mistakes were frequent reminders of the need to listen to the voice that had called and was still leading. As with all public roles, the ongoing history of those ministries will best tell the story.

HAVE I ACTED WITH INTEGRITY?

Integrity in medical terms means that the body parts and organs are working together in harmony. So it is with personal integrity. It doesn't come easily. Dishonesty and deceit push their coaxing noses in under the door. While in principle we reject them as an option, there are times we are tempted to open the door.

The question is not, Do we always act with integrity? We don't. But rather, do we, in the course of leading, correct any less-than-honest tendencies that infect ourselves and others?

In the course of planning and executing, is there a close, trusted confidant to whom you can describe what is going on and from who you will get wise counsel? Integrity is a human condition that doesn't come into play by getting up in the morning. It requires attention and diligence.

A lack of integrity sets up agitation within self, producing a wobbly instability that marginalizes your ability to think, judge, and act with clarity.

What, in leadership, needs integration so as to achieve integrity? Four essential elements: self, mission, strategies, and relationships.

We begin with *self*. It is within one's mind, character, choices, and behavior that the integrating forces are managed. We acknowledge we have flaws. There will be times when our leadership is out of line with what the assignment calls for. We and those we lead need to accept this as a given, not to whitewash realities but accept them. *Self* is the control room that manages integrity.

Surrounding *self* are essential elements that contribute to integrity: mission, strategies, and relationships.

Mission defines your identity, goals, and purpose. If one's mission is unclear, leading will be blurred. As I earlier noted, a clear mission pulls people into the endeavor or pushes them out, starting with the leader's own mission.

Strategies define what is to be done within timelines. People are drawn into the vision not just by its overarching idea but by the specific objectives you seek to reach.

Relationships with primary and secondary personnel are where mission and strategies find their actual doing. You may have a dynamic and clear mission with well-designed strategies, but without people working in healthy relationships, you may achieve some elements of the mission but the operation will lack integrity; and without integrity, the internal elements of the operation will grind against each other, agitating and wearing each other thin to the breaking point.

HAVE I CONTRIBUTED TO THE WELL-BEING OF OTHERS?

Over the past years, "servant leadership" has become a popular term, an assumed Christian maxim to describe leadership. Jesus makes clear that Christians are to serve others. Leaders do best when they lead with a heart to serve. It is good ethics and good business.

However, be wary of maxims. They carry with them an essential truth, but collect fuzzy and romantic ideas that may create wrong and unhealthy expectations. Serving others too often assumes that I serve the interests that others define.

In seeking to learn how to contribute to others' well-being, I look for outcomes that lift others in their circumstances, occupations, families, and spirit. Seeking to enhance the well-being of another assumes I understand what that well-being is. Not that leaders become parents, but we are charged with finding ingredients that enable people.

Guiding others involves at least these four components.

Discovering the gifts of your people

This will be critical to harmonious relations and success. Finding the right people, or as Jim Collins phrased it in *Good to Great*, getting "the right people on the bus," is a working metaphor identifying the value and importance of bringing together a team with potential.

Making the assignment clear and doable

I know that some on my teams have failed because I didn't provide suffi-cient lucidity in their assignments. Some might not have succeeded even with clarity, but in other cases, both I and they were less than clear. An assignment with precise goals and agreed-on expectations gives you the framework in which evaluation can more effectively occur.

Giving them space

How much space? Figuring this out is more on the "felt" than "telt" side of management. What I do know is that it is somewhere between being a micromanager and an absentee landlord. Figure it out with the team. Work from the seat of your own style and need. If you tend to lead from 33,000 feet, put in markers and dates that ensure you observe, encourage, ques-tion, and are present. If you like to get your hands into the details, work out with your team what space they need so they don't feel they are being stalked. This isn't easy to balance. In a review by my leadership team, one said I was dictatorial and another evaluated me as being too pastoral. Sometimes you can't win.

Providing evaluation

Put in place the times and means by which each person will be evaluated. Create a form of evaluation that has a high level of objectivity and is writ-ten with clear objectives of the assignment. One method is the 360 degree format, in which people are evaluated by members of the team and others with whom they work. This provides feedback as to how the person is per-ceived by others. This, as any tool, has limited value, so be careful not to hand over to an administrative person what needs doing by the leader.

HAVE I DONE WHAT I SET OUT TO DO?

This question one asks about any period of life. Goals change, but we carry our core objectives, desires, and personality into all we do. Even so, the question is important in that it calls me to consider, What am I trying to do?

Nehemiah had a clear goal, and in the end he could make his assessment. The biblical story suggests he allowed nothing outside of his objective to interrupt.

Life is relative to what each of us understands and sees. What we believe depends on what we experience, not unlike the metaphorical three blind men who were asked to touch a part of an elephant and then describe— without knowing it was an elephant—what it was they touched. One stroked a leg and proclaimed it was a tree. Another felt its trunk and said it was a hose. Another touched the tail and said he was sure it was a rope.

The usual interpretation of this story is that nothing is true. Because it makes it appear that truth depends on each person's perception, the conclusion is that all truth is relative.

How wrong this interpretation is. What we forget is that while each blind man believed an elephant was one thing or another, depending on what *he experienced,* there was standing alongside them a person who was not blind, one who saw what others didn't, who saw the entirety. It may have appeared as various things to those who felt with their hands, but that was perception, not reality. It was, after all, an elephant.

Leadership is knowing what I'm intent on doing. We don't always see the whole elephant. When we built up the EFC as a national association for evangelicals in Canada, only years later did we realize the importance of establishing a national presence in our nation's capital, Ottawa. We learned its importance as we went along. Unexpected realities show up, forcing a change in plans.

HAVE I LEFT THE PROJECT STRONGER THAN WHEN I BEGAN?

Leading is about taking an idea or organization and moving it along the avenue of effectiveness. To do that, identify the core elements, have a clearly defined mission, perpetually work on building the strength and competence of staff (and volunteers), ensure you have able governance, build fiscal stability, build a good reputation, have your strategic plan, and constantly redevelop the means of mission.

Measurement can be made in a few ways.

◆　What have been the results?

◆　Was I able to hold in tension what I thought and how I acted?

- Was I able to change myself, overcoming tendencies to acquiesce to the status quo?

- Have I empowered others?

- Did I operate with the assumption that what I needed could be learned?

- Did I hold conflicting ideas together in creative tension?

HAVE I USED MY ALLOTTED TIME WELL?

In the 1970s, time-management courses became the rage. I shunned them, concluding that learning about micromanaging was of little value. I suspect I was the loser for not attending such workshops.

Time is a gift of creation, external yet part of who we are. We make the mistake of thinking of time as linear, a series of unending seconds, minutes, hours, days, weeks, months, years stretching out to death.

Five years ago today, what were you doing? What mattered then? Unless it is memory marked (something very important happened), you probably can't recall. That day, like today, is squashed into other days. Anxieties, drivenness, unanswerable questions pushing you that day are now forgotten. The passing of time has a way of getting lost in the accumulation of days.

Time is not a bureaucratic nicety of noting when we begin and end an activity. It is a gift, as essential to our being as breath, a resource enabling the building of ideas, relationships, and enterprises. Time is not something we need to manage so much as understand and live in as part of the creative process. Modern organization demands we match jobs to the amount of time required. Salaries, even if not hourly based, are compensation for our time as well as our skills. Time becomes a tool for management. Leaders effectively use it as a device to organize. And it is a good tool.

But for leaders, time is an accommodating and nurturing environment, an essential ingredient of human makeup. It is not a taskmaster. It is not something of which we have too little. It is a friend and in sufficient supply. We don't exist for it. There is nothing intrinsically important about one moment over another. Like the physical creation, it provides an essential element in which those in God's image live out their calling. Time is part of who I am.

Time is on our side. It is within that framework we lead. Although labor laws and employment contracts specify hours to be worked, those who excel will not limit the time in which they think, pray, and work out ideas.

When we speak of managing our time, we speak of the now and the future: how we use time allocated for today and how we will organize what is coming. The past, our history, we remember and reflect on to gain perspective to guide us in decisions and to identify who we are and what our organization is today and might be tomorrow.

Time also is transcendent, becoming one with the eternal. Our lives merge into the eternal, reminding us that what we do in time has consequences out into eternity. How we and our people use time is to be seen within that larger reality and not as a measurement to fill out boxes on time sheets.

Yet the careful use of time matters. Nehemiah knew that the protection of the Temple and city was urgent. Enemies were plotting: time mattered. When I arrived to a closed-down Tyndale on June 28, 1995, we had 60 days to get it up and running for opening day. If we hadn't met critical deadlines all could have been lost.

Time awareness allows the leader to do several things:

- ◆ describe what will come to be

- ◆ provide a space of time in which the idea can reasonably be worked out

- ◆ identify what needs to be done by whom and when

- ◆ measure progress

INSIGHTS FOR SUCCESS

Lessons come by way of failure and success. Nehemiah provides us with a universal example of what is needed to move from idea to reality, from brokenness to wholeness, from scattered people to coordinated community, from living under siege to celebrating success. In this story there are rich resources as you think and plan.

FUEL HOPE

When rebuilding, adrenalin provides raw energy and feelings of possibility. But that won't last forever. In time, the glow of rescuing recedes into dull amber. What then is the lasting factor that lifts our spirit and energizes a community?

It is hope, an eternal optimism staring down imposing issues. Hope refuses to blink. Hope breeds hope. There is a disingenuous line: *Fake it until you make it*. At first it sounds as if one is being phony. But we can take another application: in moments of tension, fear, and conflict, speak hope, and as you do, hope will rise, becoming the tangible element.

REMIND YOURSELF OF THE GRANDER VISION

Work among the details; don't sleep among them. Keep your dreams for the grander vision. You won't want to leave details alone, for they are the linking fibers of the leader's agenda. Rather, from time to time, deliberately push them aside and dream the "what ifs." Do it alone. Do it with your team.

CULTIVATE CREATIVITY

Bureaucracy dulls the edge, rubbing the sharpness off curiosity and new ideas. Creativity needs affirmation, investment, and applause.

EXPECT STRESS

Stress can be an elixir. A stimulant. It keeps you on your toes. It also can kill. Look it in the face. Refuse to bow to its burden. Make it your friend, not your foe.

TEST FAITH

Push your organization to the edge, where walking in faith becomes the way forward. Christian faith is based on a life-and-death proposition: life is to be lived with a loving and interfacing God. Force your group to look over the edge, knowing God is walking alongside.

REFRESH BELIEF

Religious organizations have a tendency to focus on their dutiful exercise of religious form. This can be good, yet dangerous. Dangerous when it becomes a rote mantra devoid of life. Good when it refreshes and reminds us of the life and calling of a God of love, mercy, and grace.

BRING TRANSFORMATION

In Plato's allegory of a cave, prisoners are chained so that all they see is what is in front of them. One escapes and discovers that what he and his prisoner colleagues had believed to be true was wrong. He desperately tries to convince them but is unable.

Leaders sometimes deal with people who are so convinced of one reality that they are unable to shift their perspective. Some prefer the known, even when it is debilitating or unproductive.

Among the many opportunities a leader has, few are greater than to bring personal transformation to those with potential for good if they could but see that their current situation is a delusion. As someone who has seen a world outside of the "cave," help others see a different reality.

TELL THE STORY OF YOUR BECOMING

While it may be firmly in your mind, don't assume others are up to speed.

◆ ◆ ◆

In my final months at Tyndale, the board engaged a firm to help in the search for the next president. The representative asked, "What is a primary task of president?" My response: "Be a storyteller." The leader is charged with telling the story again and again: where we have been, where we are going, and what drives us to get there.

People love stories. Staff and board want to hear their part in it. We had come through a disaster. Though few of the former board and staff remained, our constituency and remaining faculty remembered it well. As we were freed from debt, and with a new campus coming into play, the story gained momentum. Members were enthused about this new history being written, believing this was the right course. The new story overtook the old one.

When queried about the bold new move, I would ask, "If we miss this opportunity, how will the next generation view us?" We need to see today through the eyes of the next generation.

Once we decided that the purchase of the new campus was critical to our longer term plans, the purchase price—even though considerably below market price—was an enormous challenge. We pondered the amount.

Would we inflict damage on the organization if we went forward and then couldn't meet it?

Then we asked, If we back off because of the amount, what will our grand-children think as they drive by this spectacular site and remember their grandparents backed off because they weren't sure it could be done?

That galvanized our resolve. Looking today through the eyes of the next generation helps us see what needs doing today, pulling people out of their current sphere of vision to see their world in a new way. Such teaching moments can be transformative.

◆ ◆ ◆

Nehemiah got the wall built, secured the community, constructed an ethical framework, and renewed the spiritual vision and well-being of a people, setting loose a new generation of faith and hope. It can be done. Broken walls are places where we can build new and vigorous communities of faith and life. Look for them. Let your vision for their renewed life coalesce others, so in the doing of good together, lives are transformed, made alive by the same Spirit that calls you into action.

Index

A

Aaron, 124
ability, 25, 26
Abraham, 68, 70, 74, 75
accountability, 105, 106, 147
achievement, evaluating, 153, 164
adaptability, 106, 113
admitting mistakes, 146
advocate, as type of leadership, 33
Allen, Norm, 49, 95
ambiguity, 113
apologist, as type of leadership, 34
Artaxerxes, 18, 20, 21
art of leadership, 143
the ask, 130
assignment, 147, 158
assumptions, 146, 147
Athens vs. Jerusalem, 65, 66, 81
authority, 147

B

Bastian, Donald, 15
belief, 66, 67, 162
Berlin Wall, 141
Bible college movement, 89
biblical knowledge, 78

Birch, Ken, 15, 39
Blackwell, Bishop, 38
boards
    and fund-raising, 131
    and relationship to manage-
    ment, 142, 143, 145, 146
Bojaxhiu, Mary Teresa, 61
Bonhoeffer, Dietrich, 62
boredom, 96
Bowker, Mel, 30
Bright, Bill, 45
broken wall
    finding, 40, 42
    ministry concept, 28
Buller, Herb and Erna, 15
burnout, 96
Burtchaell, James Tunstead, 92

C

calling
    faithfulness to, 154, 156
    and gifts, 34, 41
    identifying, 34, 36, 40, 42
    internal and external, 154
Cantelon, Jim and Kathy, 47, 48
Carey, William, 62

Carter, Nick, 104
Casey, Constance, 57
cave, 163
CEOs, and fund-raising, 131
change
 speed of, 141
 willingness to, 113, 140, 141
chaos, 43, 59
Christian Life Assembly, 27
Circles of Support, 24
collaboration, 144
Collins, Dave, 38
Collins, Jim, 157
conflict resolution, 145
connections, 125, 128
consultation, 41
context, of planning, 107
Cooley, Bob, 145
counselor, as type of leadership, 33
creativity, 162
crisis
 identifying importance, 98
 identifying resources, 97, 98
 as opportunity, 96, 99
 parts to be laid aside, 98
 and vision, 49
criticism, 54, 145
Cyrus, 18

D

Darius, 18
Davey, Earl, 150
David, King, 46
defined assignment, 147
delegation, 92, 95
Diana, Princess, 61
Dillard, Annie, 101
dreams
 and ability, 26

and leadership, 37
and vision, 26, 44
dynamics, of politics, 144, 147
148, 149

E

echo, 126, 127
effectiveness, measuring, 159, 160
elephant, 159
elevator speech, 129
empowerment
 of personnel, 148
 and vision, 51
encouraging/motivating, gift of, 31
Engstrom, Ted, 91
Epp, Jake, 150
Esther, Queen, 18
ethnic vote, 151
ethos, 107
evaluating achievement, 153, 164
Evangelical Fellowship of Canada
 calling to, 24, 27, 28
 essential resources, 97, 98
 and faith, 75
 fund-raising, 121, 122
 mission, 83, 85
evangelism, 30, 31
Evans, Bob, 45
evil, 143
existential resistance, 89, 90
Expo 73, 102
Ezra, 18

F

faith
 as action, 77
 and biblical knowledge, 78
 as characteristic of leadership, 71
 discerning, 80, 81

exercise of, 78, 80
and fund-raising, 131
and history of trust, 77
and humility, 80
importance of, 71, 76
and inner conviction, 77
and insecurity, 75
and interactivity with God,
71, 73, 76
and learning, 78
meaning of, 68, 71
and new realities, 76
and planning, 79
as preparation, 76
and scripture, 80
and scrutiny, 80
and Spirit's agenda, 79
testing, 162
transformative power of, 73, 74
ultimate value of, 81
and vision, 74
as way of life, 80
and wider scene, 81
workings of, 76, 78
faithfulness, 154, 156
fallout, 142
Falwell, Jerry, 84
fatigue, 96
Faught, Harry, 28
fear, 65
financial portfolio, 118
focus, and vision, 54
Ford, Leighton, 148
Franklin, John, 39
fundamentalism, 84
fund-raising
the ask, 130

benefits of leader involvement,
125, 129
boards, 131
CEOs, 131
go-away money, 129
and heart transformation,
121, 122
as inspiration to staff, 127
and larger issues, 129
and leadership, 121, 129
as litmus test, 124
and mission, 129
objections to, 122, 124
and other support, 129
and pastors, 131
storytelling, 130, 131
and trust, 129
Tyndale University College &
Seminary, 125, 126, 128 132,
133
G
Gasque, Ward, 39
gifts
and boredom, fatigue, burnout,
96
and calling, 34, 41
categories of, 33, 34
list of, 31, 32
and passion, 29, 30
Romans 12:6-8, 31
understanding, 29, 34
vision, 45, 46
giving
as encouragement, 119, 120
as extension of donor, 120
importance of, 118, 120
giving, gift of, 32

goals
    accomplishment of, 158, 159
    and calling, 42
    vs. mission and vision, 138
    Nehemiah, 158, 159
    and politics, 140
    short-term, 87
    and value proposition, 8187
    writing, 101
go-away money, 129
GOST outline, 108, 138
Graham, Billy, 23, 38, 45, 54, 90
groups within the organization, 142

H

Hagberg, J., 65
Harris, Thomas, 155
hearing. *see also* listening
    defined, 25
    and God's leading, 34
    and listening, 29
    and opportunity, 43
    and skills, 29
    training, 36, 37
Hearn, Tim, 60
heart, 118, 119, 121, 122
Heifetz, Ron, 106, 140
Henderson, Eileen, 24, 25
Hill, Jim, 15
hiring, 93
HIV/AIDS, 47, 48
Hoffer, Eric, 55
Holy Spirit
    and faith, 79
    and value proposition, 96
    and vision, 54, 55
hope
    and faith, 66, 67

fueling, 161, 162
    and who you are, 43
Hubley, Steve, 114
humility, 61, 62, 80
Hybels, Bill, 52

I

imago Dei, 72
improvisation, 143
inertia, 75
inner conviction, 77
integrity, 156, 157
Isaac, 74

J

jazz, 143
Jonas, George, 23
Joshua, 68, 70, 132
Jost, Don, 15

K

Kennedy, John F., 138
Kessler, Jay, 37
King, Martin Luther, 76
Koestenbaum, Peter, 88, 112

L

Lamott, Anne, 70
Lau, Elie, 148
Law, Terry, 83
leaders
    categories of, 33, 34
    traits of, 34
leadership
    accountability, 147
    as art, 143
    assignment, 147
    and authority, 147
    conditions for, 147, 148
    defined, 121

and dreams, 37
and empowerment, 148
and faith, 71
and fund-raising, 121, 129
and influence, 112
and integrity, 156, 157
leading vs. driving, 88
"learned" leaders, 56
and mission, 124
and politics, 137, 144
and recruiting, 117, 133
and results, 112
as science, 143
screening, 93
and self-fulfillment, 155
as servant, 129, 130, 157
as shepherd, 129, 130
strategy vs. intuition, 91
and value proposition, 91, 92
leadership team, 148, 149
leading, gift of, 32
"learned" leaders, 56
learning
    by doing, 113
    in fund-raising, 128
    from others, 78, 113
Lewis, C.S., 49
life balance, 113
Ling, Winston, 115
Linsky, Marty, 140
listening. see also hearing
    and ability, 25, 26
    the art of, 26, 29
    for opportunity, 24
    training, 36, 37
litmus test, 124
Loney, Don, 15
lowest-hanging fruit, 87

Lowney, Chris, 128

M

Macdonald, Sir John A., 44
management balance, 158
Mandela, Nelson, 43
Mathewson, Bruce, 15
McLean, Archie, 15, 49, 58
metanoia, 90
ministry, categories of, 33, 34
mission
    defining, 83, 85
    EFC, 83, 85
    elevator speech, 129
    vs. goals, 138
    and hiring, 93
    and integrity, 156
    and politics, 139, 140
    renewal of, 93
    and resources, 129
    and spiritual drift, 92
    and value proposition, 86
    vs. vision, 138
    YFC, 90
mistakes, admitting, 146
Moltmann, Jurgen, 43
money, 118. see also fund-raising;
giving; resources
Moore, Geoff, 15, 23, 154
Moral Majority, 84
Morgentaler, Henry, 85
Moses, 124
Mosteller, Sister Sue, 59
Mother Teresa, 61
motivation, and vision, 52
Muriel, nee Stiller, 77
Myatt, Sister Margaret, 59
Myra, Harold, 54

N

National Association of
    Evangelicals in, 41, 98
Nebuchadnezzar, 18
negotiation, 145
Nehemiah
    achievement, 163, 164
    and faith, 70, 76, 78
    and goals, 158, 159
    inspiration from, 28
    and leadership evaluation, 154
    and opposition, 88
    planning, 102, 103, 105, 108, 111
    and politics, 135
    resource development, 117, 118
    skills and passion, 29
    story of, 17, 21
    and vision, 45, 53, 55
networks, 128
Neufeld, John, 15
Niebuhr, Reinhold, 62
Nouwen, Henri, 59

O

Ockenga, Harold, 45
Ontario Bible College/Ontario
    Theological Seminary. *see also*
    Tyndale University College &
    Seminary
    calling to, 38, 40
    early indication of trouble, 23
    value proposition, 89
Operation Restore, 114
opportunity
    in crisis, 96, 99
    recognizing, 23, 24, 43, 63
Opportunity International, 35
opposition
    fear of, 105

as indicator, 88
and politics, 140, 144
relationship with, 144
spiritual, 143
optimism, 43, 162

P

pacing of work, 141
Paderewski, 26
pain, and vision, 48, 49
passion
    and calling, 40
    and gifts, 29, 30
    and planning, 101, 115
    and vision, 61
pastor/minister
    and fund-raising, 131
    as type of leadership, 33
Patterson, Joni, 150
The Peoples Church, 44
personal investment, 125
personality clashes, 144, 145
personnel
    accountability, 147
    defined assignment, 147
    and empowerment, 148
    evaluating, 158
    groups within, 142
    management of, 157, 158
    recruiting, 105, 157
    in time of crisis, 141
Peterson, Oscar, 143
Pierce, Bob, 34, 45, 79, 91
planning. *see also* strategic planning
    framework for, 107, 108
    and passion, 101, 115
Plato's cave, 163
player, 152

politics
    "dirty", 144
    dynamics of, 144, 147, 148, 149
    explained, 135, 136
    and goals, 140
    and leadership, 137, 144
    leadership team, 148, 149
    and mission, 139, 140
    negotiation, 145
    and Nehemiah, 135
    presence of, 136, 137
    and strategy, 140, 144
    and values, 139
    and vision, 138, 139
preaching, 95
priorities, and vision, 52, 53
psychodynamic resistance, 88
purpose, and vision, 51, 52

R

Rawlyk, George, 49
Reagan, Ronald, 84
recruiting
    funds. see fund-raising;
    resources
    and leadership, 117, 133
    personnel, 105, 157
Redekop, John, 15
Reimer, Donald, 41
relationships
    and integrity, 156
    management/board, 131,
    142, 143, 145, 146
    with personnel, 157
religious form, 162
Rendle, Hugh, 60
research, 107

resistance
    existential, 89, 90
    as indicator, 88
    and politics, 140, 144
    psychodynamic, 88
    systemic, 89
resources. see also fund-raising;
    recruiting
    and calling, 42
    identifying, 97, 98
    and larger issue, 129
    lowest-hanging fruit, 87
    and mission, 129
    short-term vs. long-term, 87
    storytelling, 130, 131
    and trust, 129
    and vision, 53
risk, 65, 71, 73, 129, 140

S

sacrifice
    in giving, 125, 126
    and vision, 57, 63
Saint-Exupéry, Antoine de, 117, 133
Saunders, Mervin, 28
Schaeffer, Francis, 37, 38
schedule, 96, 101, 105, 126
science of leadership, 143
scripture, and faith, 80
seeing, and opportunity, 43
self, 156
self-fulfillment, 155
servant leadership, 129, 130, 157
serving/helping, gift of, 31
serving/helping, and strategic planning, 113
Setter, Al, 15
Shanahan, Mike, 52
shepherd, 129, 130

showing mercy, gift of, 32
Sisters of St. Joseph, 58, 61, 132, 133
skills, and passion, 29, 30
Smith, Fred, 54
Smith, Lynn, 39, 68
Smith, Oswald J., 44, 45
The Solemn Assembly, 97
Sorbara, Greg, 151
space program, 138, 140
Spaetzel, George and Pauline, 28
speaking, gift of, 31
Spirit. *see* Holy Spirit
spiritual core, 94
spiritual drift, 92
spiritual life, 92, 94
spiritual opposition, 143
Stanley, Andy, 43, 53, 56
status quo, 141
Stemmler, Nita, 144
Stiller, Brian
    EFC, 27, 28, 47, 75, 83, 95, 97, 98
    independent evangelism, 30, 31
    learning to listen, 37, 38
    Tyndale University College &
    Seminary, 38, 40, 49, 50, 56,
    58, 61, 68, 95, 96, 114, 115,
    132, 133, 150, 152, 153, 154,
    163, 164
    vision, 47, 48
    YFC, Montreal, 24, 73, 74
    YFC, national, 24, 91, 92, 94,
    95, 102
    YFC, Toronto, 24
Stiller, David, 34, 36, 114, 120
Stiller, Jill, 34, 35
Stiller, Lily, 30, 40, 41, 58, 126, 154
Stiller, Murray, 39
storehouse of the Lord, 131

storytelling, 130, 131, 144
strategic planning
    and accountability, 105, 106
    adaptability, 106
    beginning, 106, 108
    explained, 103, 104
    GOST outline, 108
    importance of, 101, 103
    and integrity, 156
    and Nehemiah, 108, 111
    and politics, 140, 144
    in real life, 108, 112
    and recruiting, 105
    requirements for, 106, 112, 114
    and schedule, 105
    SWOT, 107
    Tyndale University College &
    Seminary, 111, 112, 114, 115
    value of, 104, 106
stress, 162
stretching, 127
success
    defining, 153, 154
    insights for, 161, 163
    measuring, 154, 161
support group, 42, 56, 95, 96, 144
Swift, Jonathan, 43
SWOT, 107
Sylvester, Mel and Marion, 15, 27, 56
systemic resistance, 89

T

teaching
    gift of, 31
    and strategic planning, 113
    as type of leadership, 33
team dynamics, 148, 149
temperature, 140
Templeton, Charles, 90

thinking, 112, 114
time-management, 160, 161
Touchstone Ministries, 49
town hall meetings, 141
Toycen, David, 92
transformation, 163
treasure, 118, 119
Trinity Western University, 27, 39
Trottman, Dawson, 45
trust, 129, 131
Tyndale University College &
    Seminary
    achievements, 153, 154
    calling to, 38, 39
    crisis as opportunity, 98, 99
    early indication of trouble, 26
    education degree, 150, 152
    and faith, 68
    fund-raising, 125, 126, 128,
    132, 133
    gift of exact amount, 119, 120
    importance of, 49
    and loss of vision, 95, 96
    Sisters of St Joseph campus,
    58, 61, 132, 133
    The Solemn Assembly, 97
    storytelling, 163, 164
    strategic planning, 111, 112,
    114, 115
    vision, 138, 139

U

U.S. space program, 138, 139
Understanding Our Times, 47
unfaith, 101
Useem, Michael, 43

V

value proposition
    building on, 92, 99
    discovering, 83, 99
    of EFC, 83, 85
    essence of, 86
    hiring, 93
    and leadership, 91, 92
    and mission commitment, 93
    and resistance, 88
    and short-term goals, 87
    and Spirit's guidance, 86
    and spiritual life, 92, 94
    and vision, 94, 96
    of YFC, 91, 92
values, and politics, 139
vision
    from within, 47
    alignment with Spirit's agenda,
    54, 55
    beyond oneself, 58
    and chaos, 49
    confirmation, 56
    cultivation of, 94, 96
    defining, 55
    development of, 47, 48
    and dreams, 26, 44
    effects of, 50, 55
    empowering, 51
    evaluating, 62, 63
    and focus, 54
    fulfillment of, 55, 62
    as gift, 45, 46
    giving purpose, 51, 52
    vs. goals, 138
    and hard work, 57
    and humility, 61, 62
    lifting hearts, 50, 51

loss of, 94, 96
maturing, 54
vs. mission, 138
and moral conviction, 58
motivating, 52
and opportunity, 43
and pain, 48, 49
and passion, 61
and politics, 138, 139
and priorities, 52, 53
and resources, 53
and sacrifice, 62
as service, 46
specificity, 104
testing, 55, 56
Tyndale University College &
Seminary, 138, 139
value of, 62, 63
what ifs, 162
workability, 104

W

Walters, Vince, 15
weaknesses, identifying, 105

well-being of others, 157, 158
what ifs, 162
Whitt, Ruth, 132
wider view, 145
Wiebe, Phil, 27, 28
Wilberforce, William, 44, 46
Wildeboer, Henry, 15, 126
Willard, Larry, 114, 120
Winter, Terry, 124
World Evangelical Alliance, 27
World Vision, 91, 92

X

Xerxes, 18

Y

Youth for Christ
calling to, 24
and loss of vision, 94, 95, 102
ministry in Montreal, 73, 74
rebirth of, 90, 91

Z

Zander, Benjamin, 43
Zerubbabel, 18

CASTLE QUAY BOOKS